Chris McLaughlin

asthma and allergies

Recipes and Advice to Control Symptoms

food solutions

TED SMART

asthma and allergies

Recipes and Advice to Control Symptoms

food solutions

Executive Editor – Jane McIntosh
Assistant Editor – Sharon Ashman
Art Director – Keith Martin
Executive Art Editor - Mark Winwood
Book Design – Birgit Eggers
Picture Research – Rosie Garai and
Zoë Holtermann
Production – Lucy Woodhead

First published in Great Britain in
2000 by Hamlyn, a division of
Octopus Publishing Group Limited,
2–4 Heron Quays, London E14 4JP

Copyright © Octopus Publishing
Group Limited 2000
ISBN 1 85613 737 6

This edition produced for
The Book People Ltd,
Hall Wood Avenue,
Haydock,
St Helens WA11 9UL

Printed in China

contents

asthma and allergies

RIGHT: Allergic conditions have become increasingly common in many countries in the last 20–30 years.

Allergy plays a part in causing the symptoms of almost all children and about half of the adults who suffer from asthma. **Like other allergic conditions, such as hay fever and rhinitis, asthma is becoming more common**, especially in better-off societies where other once-widespread illnesses such as typhoid and cholera have succumbed to improvements in living and health care standards. It would seem that something in our way of living is contributing to the rise in the number of people who suffer from allergy-related conditions, triggering a host of unpleasant and, in some cases, potentially fatal responses. Many of the most common environmental factors are already well known, although the mechanisms involved are still under scientific investigation.

Pollution, the increasing use of chemicals, the introduction of new crops such as oil seed rape, and even central heating may be contributing to the rise in allergic illnesses. **Food is one of many elements which could be playing an active part in triggering symptoms**, at least in a proportion of those affected.

Although there are, as yet, no cures for these conditions and no way of preventing them, **there is much that you can do for yourself or your child to help control symptoms** and ensure that they disrupt everyday life as little as possible. The priority is for you and your medical advisers to identify what factors in your environment are responsible for triggering your symptoms and to do everything possible to minimize contact with them. For some people, this will include making adjustments to their diet and this book explains how to find out whether this might help you and, if so, how to go about it. While lifestyle changes can make a big difference, everyone with asthma and many of those with other allergy-related symptoms will also benefit from treatment with one or more of the huge range of drugs designed to prevent and treat symptoms. In this book, you will find clear explanations of the different types of drug treatment, what they

RIGHT: There are many drugs available to help ease the symptoms of allergic responses, such as itchy, watery eyes.

FAR RIGHT: Children are more prone to suffer from asthma than adults.

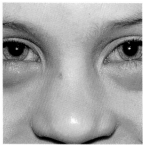

are designed to do and how to use them effectively. You will also find out about **self-help techniques** aimed at improving the way you handle stress and other lifestyle factors which may be aggravating your symptoms. You may also want to consider whether **complementary therapies** have anything to offer in your particular situation – especially by giving you better control of your breathing or helping you to relax. Here you will find explanations to enable you to select the ones that will suit you best.

Many people with allergic asthma and some of those with conditions such as hay fever and perennial rhinitis are more prone than other people to **food allergies and intolerance**. If you know or suspect that diet plays a part in triggering your symptoms, there is advice on how to identify the culprits using an elimination diet without putting your overall nutrition at risk. Once you have identified the problem foods or ingredients, you can experiment with some of the recipes which have been specially selected to exclude common allergens while guaranteeing that your meal times will be a pleasure rather than a penance. Even if your diet is not directly responsible for your symptoms, a healthy eating plan which includes the right nutrients will not only boost your general well-being and resistance to infection but may also play a part in suppressing the inflammatory response which underlies many of the symptoms of asthma and other allergic conditions.

Overall, **the aim of this book is to increase your understanding of the factors which play a part in causing your symptoms so that you can take action to minimize their effects**. By taking responsibility for your own health in this way, you will not only be able to control your symptoms more effectively, but you will no longer feel that your condition is placing severe limitations on the way you choose to live your life.

chapter 1

When you develop symptoms because of an allergy, **your immune system – your body's defence against viruses and bacteria – is responding inappropriately to substances which are actually harmless**. The range of substances that can trigger a response is huge and many people are sensitive to more than one.

Equally, symptoms can vary in their severity. For example, skin reactions, such as hives or eczema, cause discomfort and psychological distress, rhinitis and hay fever can interfere with normal life, but asthma and severe food allergies can occasionally be life-threatening. Some people who experience allergies when young find their symptoms reduce as they get older; others develop new symptoms in later life. **However, not everyone who suffers from asthma is allergic; it is usually a factor in childhood asthma but only half of those whose asthma begins in adult life are allergic**.

This chapter explains what happens in your body when you develop an allergic reaction. It is usually possible to have tests to find out whether your symptoms are the result of an allergy. Although identifying the triggers may be a long process and may not give a complete answer, **it is vital so that you can take steps to avoid them**.

the allergic response

People who have an inherited tendency to develop allergies (see 'atopy' below left) will often start to experience symptoms relatively early in life when they first encounter the particular allergens that trigger the immune response. The higher the concentration of potential allergens (such as house dust mites, animal dander, pollens and so on), the more likely the person is to develop a condition such as asthma. It has also been shown that susceptible babies who are born between spring and mid-summer – the hay fever season – are more prone to developing pollen allergies.

The body fails to realize that these substances are harmless, and mounts a full-scale defence against them as if they were harmful viruses or bacteria. (See the box on page 11 for a description of the body's reactions.) Some of these effects occur immediately on contact with the allergen; others, particularly inflammation and resulting damage to tissues, happen more gradually over the pursuing few hours.

understanding
asthma
and allergies

atopy

Some families have an inherited tendency to develop allergies as a result of some slight change to a gene that is linked to production of immunoglobulin E (IgE) and which is passed on through the generations. This doesn't mean that you will necessarily develop symptoms as a result of this genetic inheritance because other factors also play a part, but you are more likely to do so if both your parents suffer from allergies. This tendency, known as 'atopy', may show itself in different ways: one family member may have hay fever, while another has asthma or eczema, for example, and a few unfortunate people may develop more than one condition.

RIGHT: Children are more likely to develop allergies if one or both of their parents have them, although the child's allergy may take a different form.

Once the tissues in the lungs and nose have become inflamed, they react much more easily and quickly to other environmental factors which would normally have no effect. This is why when you have asthma, an attack can be brought on by breathing in cold air, cigarette smoke or traffic fumes, for example, or by ozone or the chemicals in aerosols, even though you are not actually allergic to any of these things. If the levels of allergens in your environment continue to rise, your immune system responds by producing more mast cells (see 'the body's reaction' right) and, eventually, your body is so responsive to contact with the allergens that symptoms will still be triggered even when the levels are relatively low.

FOOD ALLERGY

Although true food allergy that triggers an immune system response is not nearly as common as allergies to airborne substances, a minority of people with asthma or other allergy-related conditions may also be allergic to one or more foods or particular substances contained in what they eat or drink. Such allergies are potentially very serious since, although the symptoms may be relatively minor to begin with, they often become progressively more severe each time you encounter the allergen, and can culminate in a life-threatening condition called anaphylactic shock (see page 30). Diet may also be implicated in triggering symptoms of asthma and rhinitis however, even though you do not have a food allergy according to the strict scientific definition. Many people are sensitive to certain foods, and identifying and avoiding these as far as possible can help to relieve symptoms (see page 64). Common problem foods include wheat, dairy products and some additives used as flavourings or preservatives.

the body's reaction

Initially, quantities of the allergy antibody immunoglobulin E (IgE) are released into the bloodstream. The antibody attaches itself to special cells called mast cells which contain histamine and other chemicals, including leukotrienes, that cause the smooth muscle around the lungs to constrict. Together these substances are responsible for many allergy symptoms, and in particular they may cause the airways in the lungs and the lining of tubes in the nose to swell and trigger asthma symptoms. Other cells called eosinophils are attracted to the mast cells, setting off the process of inflammation and making the linings of the airways in the lungs and the nose hyper-sensitive. Eosinophils and other white blood cells, called lymphocytes, are also important in setting up long-term inflammation in asthma and hay fever as well as other allergic conditions such as eczema.

asthma

There are four main symptoms that should make you and your doctor suspect that you may be suffering from asthma, although they are likely to vary in severity at different times and you may not have all of them at any one time.

THE SYMPTOMS

→ **Feeling short of breath** This sensation may develop after relatively minor exertion, such as climbing stairs, or it may come on for no apparent reason and be quite severe. If you are one of the many people whose symptoms are triggered by a particular allergen, such as cat hair, you'll feel breathless when the allergen level is particularly high – when a cat jumps on to your lap, for example.

→ **Coughing** This can be caused by your lungs attempting to expel mucus or it may be a reaction to the inflammation and narrowing in the airways of the lungs. People with asthma often find that they cough a lot at night, because they are ultra-sensitive to normal changes which occur during sleep and result in a slight narrowing of the airways.

→ **Wheezing** This whistling noise is the result of air being forced out through narrowed airways in the lungs of people with asthma. But although most people associate it with asthma, it can be caused by other conditions as well, and you can have asthma without experiencing wheeziness.

→ **A tight feeling in the chest** This happens because your lungs haven't managed to get rid of all the air inside them before you inhale more. The result is a feeling of pressure as the lungs and chest over-expand to cope with the volume of air.

hay fever

The correct medical name for hay fever is 'seasonal allergic rhinitis'. It is not caused by hay, and sufferers don't have a raised temperature. The symptoms are triggered by pollens or mould spores and the time when

BELOW: Even quite minor physical exertion can sometimes trigger asthma symptoms in some people.

your symptoms begin each year will depend on the particular type to which you are allergic. Tree pollens start to build up in mid-spring, followed by grass pollens from late spring to late summer. Some people's hay fever is the result of allergies to mould spores released by different types of fungi from late summer into the early autumn. You may be unlucky enough to react to more than one type of pollen, causing your symptoms to last for several months.

THE SYMPTOMS

→ **Sneezing and an itchy, runny nose** These are reactions to the presence of allergens, such as pollen or house dust mites, which trigger the release of histamine.

→ **Blocked nose** Histamine and other chemicals released by the allergic response cause the tissues inside your nose to swell up, resulting in an unpleasant 'stuffed up' feeling, sometimes bad enough to prevent you breathing through your nose at all.

→ **Watery, itchy eyes** Inflammation and irritation are the result of reactions to allergens in your eyes, and the tears are the body's way of trying to flush them out. Rubbing itchy eyes makes the problem worse.

perennial rhinitis

Perennial rhinitis is a similar condition to hay fever except that it can occur at any time of year, not just in the pollen season. Most sufferers are allergic to house dust mites or pets such as cats and dogs, but some people react to certain pollens as well, so that their symptoms get worse in spring and summer.

THE SYMPTOMS

The symptoms are much the same as those of hay fever, although a blocked, stuffy nose is often more of a problem for people with perennial rhinitis. Being unable to breathe through your nose can cause headaches and make it difficult to sleep, and your sense of smell may become much less sharp or disappear altogether.

sinusitis

Both hay fever and perennial rhinitis can cause the tissues inside your nose to swell so much that they block the openings leading into the sinuses – spaces in the bones in your face which are normally filled with air. As a result, bacteria may breed causing a painful infection in the sinuses.

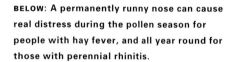

BELOW: A permanently runny nose can cause real distress during the pollen season for people with hay fever, and all year round for those with perennial rhinitis.

understanding
asthma
and allergies

BELOW: People whose hay
fever is triggered by birch
pollen may also develop a
sensitivity to hazelnuts.

BOTTOM: Alcoholic drinks
such as wine often contain
preservatives that can cause
respiratory symptoms in
people with asthma.

food and allergies –
making the connection

It is worth remembering that allergic reactions to food may be set off by breathing in tiny particles – even sitting next to someone eating peanuts can trigger symptoms in a person with a peanut allergy, for example. However, you are more likely to develop adverse effects from swallowing offending foods or drinks, even though the response may not be either immediate or obvious.

Although most doctors would accept that reactions to certain foods can play a part in triggering symptoms of asthma and rhinitis, many would claim that this is relatively insignificant, with a few important exceptions. If you are convinced that your diet does play a role in triggering your symptoms or making them worse, you may encounter a degree of scepticism from the physicians who are treating your condition.

The classic food allergy which produces swelling around the mouth and other major symptoms immediately after eating the offending food is easily recognized, but some food reactions are less dramatic and may occur some hours afterwards, making them much more difficult to identify. As well as triggering symptoms of asthma or rhinitis, problems originating in reactions to food are likely to cause other symptoms, such as abdominal pain and bowel disturbance. Keeping a detailed diary of everything you eat and drink, plus details of your symptoms, may help you to trace any link between the two (see page 70).

Apart from causing a true allergic response involving the immune system, foods can affect people with asthma and other allergy-related conditions in a number of different ways. One of the main problems is that many foods actually contain histamine, one of the chemicals released in the allergic reaction, and eating these foods in any quantity can trigger respiratory symptoms. Certain additives, mostly those used as preservatives, can make asthma worse in people who develop a sensitivity to them. The main culprits are compounds containing sulphur, which may be given off as sulphur dioxide gas and inhaled when you chew foods containing sulphur-based preservatives. Many alcoholic drinks also contain these substances. For more information on how to avoid them, see page 67.

A relatively small number of people with asthma develop a sensitivity to aspirin (see page 45), and they may also react to foods containing substances called salicylates which resemble aspirin. However, as avoiding such foods means cutting out fruit, vegetables, nuts and much more besides, the cure is worse than the disease for most people and only worth trying in the case of very severely affected individuals.

Sometimes, people who know that their symptoms are triggered by a particular allergen may find they also react to apparently very different substances. For example, people whose hay fever is triggered by birch

pollen are also often sensitive to hazelnuts and apples, while those allergic to grass or ragweed pollen may develop symptoms when they eat melon.

INTOLERANCE AND ALLERGY

Because there is no straightforward test to diagnose most suspected cases of food intolerance, its role in triggering or exacerbating symptoms is much more difficult to pinpoint. The exception is when an individual is found to lack some essential component in their digestive system that prevents them from dealing normally with certain food proteins. For example, people with coeliac disease cannot digest gluten, the protein found in wheat, while people in parts of the world where dairy products are uncommon often lose the ability to digest milk protein once they are weaned because their bodies stop producing the necessary enzyme.

People who experience food intolerance or sensitivity may react with a wide range of symptoms which often develop some time after consuming the culprit food. Generally, the food concerned is something they particularly like and therefore eat frequently and, although any food can potentially have ill-effects, those most often implicated are staples such as wheat, milk, eggs, fish and shellfish.

A small number of people only experience breathlessness and other asthma symptoms after a bout of strenuous exercise, a condition known, reasonably enough, as exercise-induced asthma, or EIA. For some reason that is not understood, some of them find that their symptoms are worse or only develop when they have eaten certain foods beforehand. Celery seems to be a major culprit in this respect, although individuals may have their own personal triggers.

understanding
asthma
and allergies

children –
taking avoiding action

If you and your partner both suffer from allergic illnesses such as asthma, hay fever or eczema, your children face a higher-than-average risk of developing a similar allergic condition (see page 10). The odds are greater still if you both have the same condition. In these circumstances, it may be worthwhile taking sensible precautions before your baby is born to improve the odds against such an allergy developing, although there are no guarantees.

In an ideal world, you would aim to give birth to your baby outside the pollen season – children born during this period appear to be more susceptible to hay fever. On a more practical level, it is worthwhile doing all you can to rid your home of potential allergens – including pets if possible – before the birth. This is especially important in the room where your baby will sleep and in the main living room. A five-year research study reported in 1999 found that babies who had become sensitized to allergens by the end of their first year of life, as shown by skin prick tests, were more likely to have developed asthma by the age of five. For details of how to reduce allergen levels in the home, see page 44.

In future, treatment designed to control the reactions of allergic mothers-to-be to allergens in the environment, especially during the second and third trimesters of pregnancy, could diminish the chances of the child developing allergies after birth. The other important step which is well worth taking is to stop smoking and to make sure no one else does so around your baby once he or she is born.

FEEDING YOUR BABY

Breast milk is the ideal food for a baby. As well as meeting all his or her nutritional needs, it can help to protect your baby by passing on the benefits of your immunity to many common infections while his or her own is still developing. Unfortunately, breast-feeding does not always come easily to many new mothers, and some give up after a few days or weeks, or choose to bottle feed from the start. Your midwife and health visitor should be able to offer good advice if you want to breast-feed, or you can contact one of the many organizations such as the National Childbirth Trust or La Leche League whose trained breast-feeding counsellors can help you to overcome any difficulties.

If you can manage to breast-feed for six months before introducing your baby to solid food of any kind, he or she may be less likely to develop allergies. If you and your partner suffer from allergic conditions, it may also be worthwhile to avoid consuming any of the most common allergy triggers while breast-feeding so that traces cannot be passed in your milk to your baby; eggs, fish, milk and dairy products, nuts, wheat and oranges are all potential culprits. However, if you do decide to do this, ask your health visitor or doctor's advice about taking supplements, especially calcium, to ensure that your diet is nutritionally sound.

When you begin giving your baby other foods besides milk, introduce new foods gradually and avoid giving any of the foods listed above as potential allergens until the baby is a year old. Don't give nuts in any form until the age of three. If you offer new foods one at a time, you will be able to see immediately if any one of them upsets the child. This will also give the baby's body time to adjust to the change in diet at its own rate. However, even if you do take all possible precautions, your baby may still develop an allergy and you cannot be blamed if this happens since there is as yet no sure way of preventing it.

WHAT KIND OF MILK?

When a baby does not seem to be doing well on a particular brand of milk formula, some parents resort to changing brands in the hope that this will improve matters. However, all ordinary formula feeds are prepared from cows' milk, so this is unlikely to work. If you are concerned that your baby may be sensitive to feeds made from cows' milk, you should consult your doctor or health visitor as to whether you might do better on one of the specially modified milks called 'hydrolysates'. These contain milk proteins which have been modified to make them less allergenic. Babies who are allergic to cows' milk are very likely to develop similar reactions to soya-based formulas and later to goats' milk. If your baby is sensitive to milk, you will need the guidance of your doctor or health visitor in managing the problem, but you may find that the sensitivity diminishes or disappears in time, so that cows' milk can be given to him or her again safely.

Although most of us are conscious of the health benefits of low-fat milk and dairy products, these are not suitable for young children who need the concentrated calories of full-fat milk to help fuel their growth and energy expenditure.

ABOVE: Breast milk is the ideal food for a young baby.

BELOW: Get expert advice before changing from one type of baby milk to another.

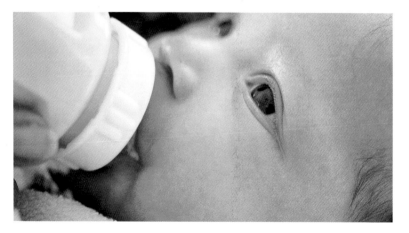

understanding
asthma
and allergies

allergic conditions –
on the increase

The last 20–30 years have seen an enormous increase in the numbers of people known to be suffering from some form of allergic illness, and surveys suggest that the rise has been most dramatic in the relatively wealthy countries of Europe and in the USA, Australia and New Zealand.

In the UK, it has been estimated that as many as one in four adults will experience an allergic reaction at some time in their lives; for around a quarter of these, this means suffering the annual misery of hay fever. There are thought to be some 3.4 million peopİe with asthma, although not all of these cases are the result of allergy. The numbers affected by various forms of atopic conditions are rising by about 5 per cent a year in the UK, and studies have shown comparable increases in other countries, including Sweden, Norway, Switzerland, Australia, New Zealand and the USA.

The proportion of the US population experiencing allergies is similar to that in the UK. Of the 40–50 million individuals concerned, some 39.5 million have hay fever and over 17 million have asthma.

Much of this rise in allergic illness has affected children predominantly; rates of asthma have doubled in many Western countries in the two decades up to 1995. Research suggests that children from poorer families in the UK develop the condition more often than those from wealthier homes; in the USA, children of African-American parents are 25 per cent more likely to develop asthma than other children. In early childhood, boys are more likely to be affected than girls, but the gap tends to close as they get older; and in the USA, the rates of asthma rose much faster in girls (81 per cent) than in boys (42 per cent) between 1982 and 1994.

LOOKING FOR EXPLANATIONS

As we have seen, people who develop allergic conditions generally do so only if they have inherited a genetic predisposition. The disease itself is then triggered by something they encounter in their environment. It seems obvious that the rise in allergic illness cannot be occurring because more people are inheriting a tendency to atopic illness; that kind of evolutionary change happens over very long periods of time, and in any case there is other evidence that changes in the environment are responsible. In particular, children who move from an area where the incidence of such illness is relatively low to one where it is high are more likely to develop an allergy than if they had stayed in their original homes.

It has also been noted that the younger children in larger families seem to be less prone to allergy than older ones or those in small families, and it has been suggested that this might be connected to the fact that they are likely to be exposed to more infections passed on by their brothers and sisters, thus strengthening their immune system. Improvements in hygiene mean children are less likely to be exposed to parasitic worm infestation – and it is the same mechanism used by the body to repel such invaders that triggers the allergic reaction. The theory is that these repeated challenges give the immune system something to 'work on', so that it is less likely to go awry and respond to normally harmless allergens.

ABOVE: The droppings of the house dust mite are one of the main allergens responsible for triggering asthma.

LEFT: Allergic conditions are on the rise in many countries, especially in children.

allergen levels

High levels of exposure to potential allergens are likely to trigger symptoms of allergic disease in those who are genetically susceptible. Changes in the way we live in many Western societies have made life more comfortable but at the same time have created the conditions in which allergens can accumulate. Central heating, double glazing and draught exclusion, fitted carpets and curtains can help to create an environment where house dust mites flourish, and fumes from gas cookers and fires cannot easily escape. If humidity levels rise, condensation may encourage the growth of mould, and as pets become ever more popular, animal allergens can be spread around the cleanest home. Most experts agree that air pollution is rarely responsible for causing allergic disease, but high concentrations of ozone, nitrogen oxides and other particles in the air can certainly trigger attacks of asthma and make other allergic symptoms worse.

It is also possible that changes in our diet may be contributing to the rise in allergic disease; in particular, the increased consumption of salty snacks and meals high in saturated fat, and the decline in the amounts of fresh fruit and vegetables may be significant (see pages 63–75).

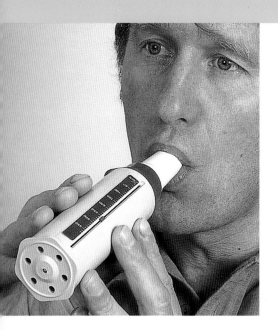

ABOVE: You may be asked to breathe into a peak flow meter if your doctor suspects that you have asthma.

what to tell the doctor
Points to include, if they apply to you, are:

→ when your symptoms began
→ how they have changed over time
→ when they are most and least severe
→ what, if anything, triggers them
→ what is the usual interval between encountering a suspected trigger and symptoms starting
→ what treatment you have already tried (including complementary as well as orthodox) and what effect it has had, if any
→ The doctor will also ask about your family history, whether close relatives suffer from allergies, and about your general health and lifestyle, including your diet

how allergic illness is diagnosed

What you can tell the doctor about your condition (or that of a young child) is of vital importance in diagnosing allergy-related disease. If you feel you might not remember everything, it's worth making some notes to take with you to the consultation.

PEAK FLOW MEASUREMENT

If your symptoms suggest a diagnosis of asthma, your doctor may carry out a simple test in the surgery using a gadget called a peak flow meter. It measures the maximum speed at which you can expel air from your lungs as you breathe out, and the measurement will be compared to what is normal for someone of your age, height and gender. This is called the peak expiratory flow rate (PEFR) and is lower in people with asthma, as well as being lower in the morning than in the evening. The test is repeated after you have been given a dose of a drug designed to relieve asthma symptoms; if the result of this 'reversibility test' is better it helps to confirm that you have asthma.

SPIROMETRY

If the results of the initial tests are not clear-cut, other investigations, called lung function tests, may be arranged. These usually take place in a hospital or clinic. An instrument called a spirometer is used to assess whether the air leaves your lungs at normal speed and whether you are able to empty your lungs of air each time you breathe out. You may be asked to repeat the test after a dose of a bronchodilator drug (as with peak flow measurement) or after putting your lungs under stress. This will show whether the airways become narrower when you exercise.

ALLERGY TESTS

The details of your symptoms, plus peak flow measurement (and possibly spirometry) in the case of asthma, will usually establish whether you have a condition which is or might be caused by an allergy. The next step for some people will be tests to identify the allergens that trigger symptoms, although often the culprit will be obvious. For example, hay fever which begins in early spring is almost certainly a reaction to grass pollens, and many people already know that they are allergic to cats. However, asthma is not always an allergic response.

CAP-RAST

This is a blood test which is designed to identify specific allergens that have triggered an IgE response and can be detected in a blood sample. It may be helpful where diagnosis is otherwise difficult, especially in people with allergic skin conditions, but it is an expensive procedure and unnecessary in most cases.

FOOD CHALLENGES

Specific food allergies may not always show up in skin or blood tests, and a minority of people may need this type of test to identify the culprits. Initially, suspect foods are eliminated from the person's diet, and they are then given tastes of a number of dishes, with and without the suspect food. Ideally, neither patient nor doctor knows whether it is present and it should not be identifiable by sight or taste. However, because of the possibility of a severe reaction (anaphylactic shock – see page 30), such tests must be done in hospital in carefully controlled conditions.

skin prick testing

The fact that the mast cells to which the allergy antibody IgE binds are found in the skin as well as in your nose, mouth and lungs means that skin tests can often be used to identify the individual allergens to which your body is reacting. A small amount of a diluted allergen is dropped on to your skin (usually on your forearm) and a tiny hole is punctured in the skin below it with a fine needle or lancet. If you are allergic to the substance, a small red weal will appear at the spot, usually within 15 minutes or so. Several allergens can be tested in this way at the same time. Although useful, skin prick testing is not always reliable, especially in babies and young children, and may sometimes produce false-negative or false-positive results. In the latter case, you may have no symptoms even though the tests show your immune system does respond to the allergen.

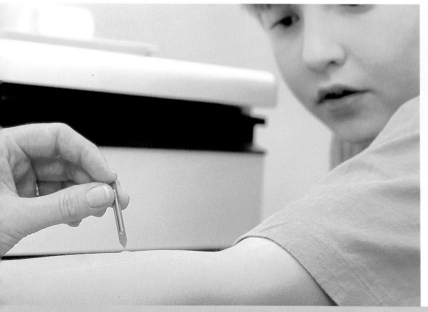

LEFT: A skin prick test, shown here, can be a useful means of establishing whether you are allergic to a specific substance or not.

In a healthy person, breathing is such a normal function that it is rarely noticed unless something disrupts it, such as getting out of breath after a sudden sprint. Yet if it stopped for more than about four minutes, damage would occur in various parts of the body and cells would start to die. **Breathing is fundamental to healthy life because it is the means by which the body is provided with essential oxygen that enables all the body cells to function**. It is also how the body gets rid of carbon dioxide, a poisonous waste product of metabolism. When all is working, the body automatically regulates its intake of oxygen and release of carbon dioxide to meet its needs.

It's almost impossible to think about anything else if you're having to make an effort to breathe. **Any illness or injury that affects your ability to breathe is serious and may be life-threatening.** The range of problems that can affect breathing is wide, partly because several different parts of the body can be affected – the nose, mouth, trachea (the passageway to and from the lungs) and the lungs themselves. **Allergic conditions can interrupt the smooth working of all these parts in a variety of ways, and understanding how this can happen is crucial to understanding and learning to cope with asthma and allergies**.

how your lungs work

As air is breathed in through the nose, it is purified and warmed before it continues its journey towards the lungs. The hairs inside the nostrils trap any large particles. The smaller ones, including many bacteria and viruses, are caught on the mucous membranes lining the nose and mouth. Tiny hairs, called cilia, propel dust and small particles down from the mucous membranes into the throat, where they are swallowed.

In order to draw air in, muscles around the ribs and in the diaphragm contract, so that the rib cage lifts up and outwards and the diaphragm drops down. This series of movements expands the chest cavity and air is drawn in to fill the space.

Air passes from the nose and mouth into a space behind them called the pharynx, then through the larynx (or voice box), where air travelling between the two membranes comprising the vocal cords enables them to vibrate and produce the sounds of speech.

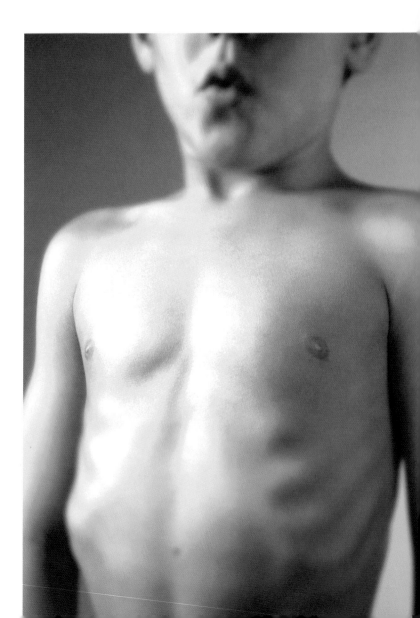

RIGHT: Allergic conditions can sometimes interfere with the respiratory system, making it difficult for a sufferer to breathe.

Until this point, the air has been moving through what's known as the upper respiratory tract. The lower respiratory tract begins just below the larynx, where it joins the trachea, or windpipe. Theoretically, only air can pass into this tube, although occasionally something 'goes down the wrong way' and triggers an automatic coughing reflex in the body's attempt to expel it.

The trachea is around 25 cm (10 inches) long in an adult and, just below the level of the breastbone, it divides into two branches going to the right and left lungs. The two bronchi (or lung airways) consist of muscle and cartilage and are lined with mucous glands. The lungs themselves are two bags, protected by the ribs and backbone and each sealed in its own airtight cavity by membranes called the pleura. Inside each lung, the bronchi divide into smaller and smaller branches, surrounded with thin layers of muscle but without the supporting cartilage that helps to keep the main bronchi open. The smallest bronchi (called bronchioles) are only 0.2 mm ($\frac{1}{125}$ inch) in diameter and each ends in a small sac containing many alveoli – pouches that fill with air. An adult has literally hundreds of millions of alveoli inside their lungs, and oxygen and carbon dioxide can pass through their very thin walls into and out of the network of small blood vessels (or capillaries) which surrounds them. In this way, oxygen can be transmitted through the arteries throughout the body and carbon dioxide can be returned via the veins to the lungs to be expelled.

BREATHING OUT

To breathe out, you relax the muscles in your diaphragm and between your ribs, your diaphragm lifts up and your rib cage moves in and down, so reducing the space inside your chest cavity. This increases the pressure inside, causing your lungs to contract and force the air out. When required, you can exaggerate this process to make the air come out faster – when blowing out candles on a birthday cake, for example. Although we think of breathing out as emptying our lungs of air, in reality a small amount remains inside – about 3 litres (5 pints) comprised of a mixture of oxygen and carbon dioxide – known as the 'residual volume'.

what's in the air?

The vital component in air is, of course, oxygen, but by the time the air reaches the air sacs in the lungs, oxygen represents only about a fifth of the total volume. The rest is made up of a tiny amount of carbon dioxide plus nitrogen. Unfortunately, when air is polluted, it may contain other substances and gases, such as ozone and by-products of internal combustion and diesel engines, for example, and some may bypass the filter system and end up in the lungs.

ABOVE: It is important for asthma and allergy sufferers to avoid air that is polluted as it has the potential to aggravate their symptoms.

what happens in asthma?

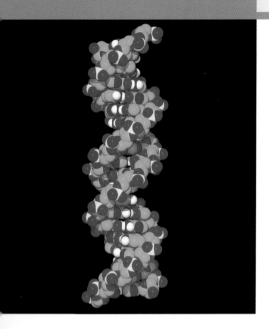

ABOVE: The famous double helix structure of a DNA molecule of which all genes are made.

Although the causes of asthma and the frequency and severity of attacks may differ from one person to another, what everyone with asthma shares is a tendency for the airways in their lungs to narrow in certain circumstances. This tendency is inherited (although genetics do not provide a complete explanation) and is often combined with a general tendency to allergic reaction. Virtually all children with asthma are allergic, although allergy accounts for only about half of the cases of asthma that develop for the first time in adulthood. In fact, even if your asthma is primarily allergic, attacks can be triggered by many different kinds of stimuli, not only allergens, including cold air, cigarette smoke, exercise, respiratory infections and, in a minority of people, by food or aspirin-type drugs.

It is thought that, in allergy-prone babies, the airways become sensitized early in life, narrowing on contact with allergens, especially the droppings of house dust mites. Once the airways become hyper-responsive (or 'twitchy'), they will narrow in the presence of lower concentrations of allergens or other irritating substances or conditions. The longer the babies remain in the presence of high levels of allergens, the more rapidly and dramatically their airways will respond to them, so that eventually symptoms may be set off even at relatively low levels.

The sensitive airways can become inflamed as the immune system tries to defend the lungs from whatever is 'attacking' them, even though the attackers are harmless to healthy people. Mucus is released by the cells lining the airways to absorb dust or other particles, so that they can then be got rid of by coughing. The muscles in and around the airways contract, causing more narrowing, in an attempt to limit the amount of offending particles coming into the lungs with the air, restricting normal breathing still more.

As anyone with asthma knows, the symptoms caused by these changes in the airways can be very frightening, especially when it is a real struggle to breathe. The instinctive reaction is to try to take in more oxygen by breathing in harder and faster, but in fact this can make the problem still worse. You end up trying to take in more air before you have properly breathed out. The air making its way to the outside can do so only very slowly because its escape route is obstructed, and the desperate attempts to draw in more air impede its progress still further. At the same time, the trapped 'used' air is making it more difficult for fresh air to get to the air sacs deep inside the lungs. What's more, the need to

ABOVE: People with asthma need to carry their reliever inhalers with them all the time in case of an attack.

accommodate extra amounts of air can cause the lungs and the whole chest region to expand beyond their normal range, and this is what causes the sensation of uncomfortable tightness, which many people describe as feeling like a tight band around their chest.

People with asthma, especially those who have identified the specific allergens that provoke their symptoms, can often recognize what happened to cause an attack and the immediate symptoms. Once the attack has subsided, they start to feel better. However, sometimes they may then find that their breathing again becomes more difficult a few hours later, and a peak flow measurement would show that their lung function has worsened. This is known as a late asthmatic response, but fortunately not everyone experiences it, and even those who do may not do so after every attack.

asthma and the mind

At one time, people with asthma were often thought of as being more neurotic than the rest of the population, leading many people to believe that they could control their symptoms if only they could learn to cope better with everyday stresses. Doctors now accept that this is both unkind and untrue. Emotional problems and stress do not cause asthma, although they may sometimes trigger an attack or make one worse in a person who already has the condition. This doesn't mean that people with asthma are any more emotionally unstable than anyone else; it is just that emotional trauma can have more significant consequences for them than for other people.

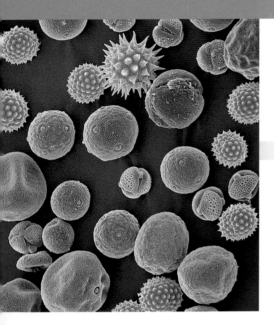

ABOVE: The immune system responds to an allergen, such as pollen, by releasing a cascade of cells to destroy the invader, and this is what causes the symptoms.

glue ear

Sometimes mucus that is blocking your nose can clog the eustachian tubes which link the nose to the middle ear. This may develop into glue ear, properly known as chronic secretory otitis media. The cavities in the middle ear, normally filled with air, become clogged with a sticky mucus which cannot escape, and hearing can be affected. This problem often affects children with bad hay fever.

what happens in other allergic conditions?

HAY FEVER

Seasonal allergic rhinitis, to give it its proper name, is the most common allergic condition and the numbers of people affected have been rising in recent years. The symptoms predominantly affect the upper respiratory tract, rather than the lungs themselves, although many people with hay fever also have asthma, and find that it gets worse during the pollen season.

When you come into contact with your particular allergens, what actually happens is that the grains of pollen or mould spores get into the eyes as well as being inhaled through the nose and mouth. Mast cells in the nose and eyes trigger the allergic reaction, releasing histamine and a chain of other chemicals which set up inflammation in the membranes lining the nose and in the eyes. The eyes become red, itchy and watery, and the tear ducts work overtime to try to wash away the allergens. Histamine and leukotrienes have a devastating effect on the nose as well: you may have long bouts of violent sneezing, copious amounts of watery fluid are secreted to clear out the offending particles and the lining of the nose may swell quite severely. At least half of all hay fever sufferers find that a blocked nose is the most annoying symptom because they have to breathe through their mouth, which consequently becomes dry, they get frequent headaches and find it difficult to sleep at night. If your nose is completely stuffed up, you may lose your sense of taste and smell as well. Because you are forced to breathe through your mouth, your nose cannot do a proper job of trapping pollens and other allergens, which exacerbates the whole problem. Pollen in your mouth can make your throat itch, and a nerve linking your throat to your ears can become irritated, so that your ears itch too.

Most people with hay fever notice that their symptoms begin as the levels of their particular allergens in the air begin to rise. This triggers the allergic reaction, and once that has been set off, you can get quite severe symptoms even when the pollen count is not particularly high. As with asthma, you may find that you then begin reacting to other 'pollutants' in the air, such as cigarette smoke. Even though you are not actually allergic to them, they easily irritate the sensitized tissues in the nose and eyes.

PERENNIAL RHINITIS

This is a year-round problem because the symptoms are triggered by a reaction to allergens that are not confined to any particular season. The most common culprits are the droppings of house dust mites as well as allergens from household pets, especially cats and dogs. However, there is an enormous range of possible triggers, and it may take considerable time and effort to identify the less common ones. Smoke from cigarettes or fires, certain foods or additives, strong perfumes and fumes, air fresheners and chemicals in household cleaning products, as well as chemicals used in the workplace, should all be considered as possible triggers, among other things.

Some people with perennial rhinitis find their symptoms worsen or change in spring and summer because they are also sensitive to one or more of the seasonal pollens. Generally speaking, perennial rhinitis causes problems in the nose more frequently than in the eyes. If you do get conjunctivitis (inflammation of the eye membranes) in addition, it suggests that the allergens triggering it are likely to be airborne.

A minority of people with perennial rhinitis find that certain foods play a part in causing or worsening symptoms, and some also react to aspirin-type drugs. For some reason, as yet unexplained, people who show this sensitivity also often develop small harmless growths in the nose called nasal polyps, which can make it difficult to breathe through the nose and affect the sense of smell.

SINUSITIS

The sinuses are cavities in the facial bones below each eye and above the middle of the eyebrows, and are linked to the nasal passage. They are normally filled with air, but if the openings become blocked with mucus or if the membranes lining them are affected by an allergic reaction, they can become inflamed or infected. The result can be a nasty headache or pain in the cheeks, and if they are actually infected, you may feel feverish and generally quite unwell.

ABOVE: Pollen grains from a wide range of trees and plants trigger hay fever symptoms when inhaled by those susceptible to them.

early signs of severe food allergy

Although it occasionally strikes without any recognized warning, many people will have had some reaction to contact with the allergen before experiencing anaphylactic shock. You should make a big effort to identify the cause of any of the following symptoms and do everything possible to avoid future contact with the suspect food.

→ tingling and swelling of the lips and tongue
→ feeling breathless
→ eruptions of weals on a large area of skin
→ any skin rash
→ vomiting

anaphylactic shock – an emergency situation

Anaphylactic shock is a very severe allergic reaction which can be fatal if the correct treatment is not given promptly. It is most often provoked by eating or even by contact with a food to which the person is allergic, but can also be triggered by bee stings or by latex (used in surgical gloves) in susceptible people. A minority of individuals with asthma develop this form of allergy, but it can also affect those who don't have other allergy-related conditions. However, while it is still uncommon, the numbers of people affected by this type of allergy do appear to be rising, particularly among children, and everyone needs to be aware of the early signs (see box left).

As far as true food allergy is concerned, peanuts are perhaps the major culprit, but other types of nut, milk, eggs, fish and shellfish are also recognized triggers in certain individuals. Peanut allergy can be a particular problem because the specific allergen can be contained in other, apparently innocent, foods and in the form of peanut (arachis) oil, which is used in some cosmetics and skin treatments. As manufacturers and food retailers have become increasingly aware of the risks of peanut allergies, they have become more diligent about including warnings on any product that might potentially trigger symptoms in susceptible people.

If you or your child have ever experienced any of the symptoms listed in the box on the left and you cannot identify what triggered them, it would be sensible to consult your doctor to ask whether skin prick testing (see page 21) would be advisable.

SYMPTOMS OF ANAPHYLACTIC SHOCK

These may come on immediately or may develop more slowly in the next hour or two after contact with the allergen. If you have asthma, you may experience the symptoms of an attack as well and emergency help is vital. As well as the symptoms listed in the box, you should always call an ambulance if you experience those in the following list, unless you have good reason to be sure they are caused by something other than a severe allergic reaction.

→ feeling dizzy, faint or weak, with a very fast pulse
→ diarrhoea, pains in the stomach or abdomen or incontinence
→ disorientation and slurring of speech
→ pallor and itchy skin
→ feeling anxious or apprehensive for no apparent reason

BELOW: Dramatic skin rashes and rapidly swelling lips could be signs of anaphylactic shock – a serious condition that needs urgent medical attention.

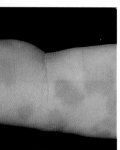
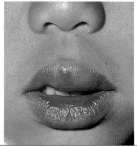

ABOVE: Put an unconscious person in the recovery position if they have vomited to prevent them inhaling any of the vomit.

FIRST AID

The first priority is to call an ambulance, or get the person to a hospital yourself if this is likely to be quicker. Unless the person concerned has been prescribed emergency treatment for self-administration, you should not give them any medication other than a reliever drug for an asthma attack. Stay with them until help comes, and keep them sitting up if their lips and tongue are swollen as it will be easier to breathe in this position. However, they may need to lie down in the recovery position if they have vomited and are losing consciousness, to prevent them inhaling any vomit.

Anaphylactic shock can be reversed effectively with the injection of corticosteroid drugs, and this will be done at the hospital. It will stop the massive release of histamine that is responsible for triggering the symptoms, and cause the blood vessels to contract, so halting the potentially lethal drop in blood pressure.

People who have had one attack of this nature (or who have had previous symptoms suggesting they may do so in the future) will usually be provided with a simple device with which they can inject themselves with adrenaline and be given instructions on when and how to use it. The usual advice is to err on the side of caution and give yourself an injection as soon as you suspect you might be going into anaphylactic shock; no harm will be done if it proves to have been a false alarm.

As yet, there is no cure for asthma or any of the other allergy-related conditions, **but with the right kind of treatment, tailored to your individual needs and adjusted as necessary, the symptoms can often be well-controlled**. As with many chronic diseases, management should be a partnership between you and your medical advisers. They depend on you to give accurate accounts of your symptoms, to take your medication as prescribed and report back on its effects – both good and bad. They should also advise and support you in making necessary adjustments to your lifestyle, in terms of diet, exercise and modifying your environment, to give prescribed medication the best chance of success.

It's a rare individual who doesn't get sick and tired of constant medication from time to time. Teenagers with asthma often rebel against using their medication in the correct way, but many adults feel much the same at times. **Allergic conditions such as asthma and hay fever may become less severe or even disappear with increasing age**, but for many people regular medication simply has to be endured. Even if your treatment works well, it's a good idea to have regular meetings with your doctors to review your condition and to keep abreast of new treatments and improvements to existing ones.

conventional treatment

drug side effects

Sodium cromoglycate-type drugs rarely have any side effects at all, although powder inhalers may make you cough; aerosol inhalers don't normally cause the same problem. Inhaled steroids in the low to moderate doses most commonly used are very unlikely to cause any major side effects, especially if you learn to use the inhaler properly so that you avoid swallowing too much of the drug. Rinsing out your mouth and throat with fresh water after each dose will help to prevent any steroid accumulating in the back of the throat, where it can otherwise cause irritation and a cough. Some people develop a tendency to thrush infections in the mouth when taking steroids, but thorough mouth rinsing is also helpful with this problem. If it persists, your doctor may recommend lozenges which inhibit the growth of the fungus that causes thrush.

If you are caring for a child with an allergic illness, it can be a heavy responsibility, particularly where asthma and severe food allergies are concerned, but the more you can learn about the condition and its treatment, the better both you and your child will cope.

It is rare to be able to avoid the allergens that trigger your symptoms altogether, so the basis of treatment will normally be to control the underlying allergic response as far as possible, combined when necessary with other medications to relieve the symptoms. Getting the right balance between these two approaches may take time and a certain amount of experimentation, so it is important not to lose patience if success does not come immediately.

asthma treatment

AN AGREED PLAN

Your doctor will discuss with you what drugs he or she is planning to prescribe and how they should be taken. It is important that you understand and are happy to follow these recommendations, so don't hesitate to ask questions or voice any concerns you may have at this stage. Either the doctor or the asthma nurse should give you a written version of your asthma management plan, detailing all the medications, doses and when to take them, plus advice on what action to take if you have an attack or your symptoms get worse. If you will be doing peak flow measurements at home, it will also give guidelines on what results to expect and what you should do if your readings vary. It may be necessary to make adjustments to your plan from time to time, depending on how you get on with the treatment. Your treatment should, in any case, be reviewed after the first 3–6 months, and it may well then be possible to reduce your drug regime if your symptoms are well-controlled.

preventers

There are various different treatments designed to reduce the inflammation in the airways which is the underlying reason for asthma symptoms. They work on a long-term basis, so you are unlikely to notice any difference when you first start using them, but it is vital to continue the treatment and take them every day, even if you have no symptoms. The types of preventer drugs used most widely are corticosteroids, and cromoglycate and nedocromil sodium, the latter two working in a similar way to one another.

RIGHT: Caring for a child with a serious allergic condition such as asthma can be worrying for parents.

CORTICOSTEROIDS

In recent years, many doctors have started prescribing inhaled steroids in low doses for most people with asthma, even those whose symptoms are relatively mild, because research has shown that they help to prevent long-term damage to the airways and make it less likely that asthma will worsen. Many people worry about taking steroids on a regular basis, either because they confuse corticosteroids with the anabolic steroids taken by some sports people to boost performance, or because they have heard about serious side effects from taking high doses of steroid tablets. Neither of these worries has any foundation. Corticosteroids are quite different from anabolic steroids, and low or medium doses of inhaled steroids have only minor, if any, side effects which are greatly outweighed by their benefits. Some people with more severe asthma may need to take steroids in tablet form, usually in short courses. They have a powerful anti-inflammatory effect, and doctors take care to monitor the balance of benefits and possible side effects in such cases.

CROMOGLYCATE-TYPE DRUGS

These are designed to prevent the allergic reaction involving mast cells from beginning when you come into contact with an allergen, and may be prescribed instead of steroid preventers, especially for children who sometimes do better on this treatment than adults. They are taken through an inhaler, and if your symptoms are mild, you may be recommended to use it only when necessary – say, before a bout of exercise. However, to benefit from their full effect as preventatives, these drugs need to be taken several times a day, and the effects will only begin to show themselves after you've been taking them for a few weeks.

The newest type of preventer treatment is a group of drugs known as leukotriene antagonists, which are available both as inhalers and in tablet form. As explained on page 11, leukotriene is one of the chain of chemicals released during the allergic response and this treatment is designed to interrupt this process and so prevent the airways from becoming inflamed.

relievers

By far the most common drugs used to ease asthma symptoms are the group known as ß-2 (pronounced 'beta two') relievers. They are almost always given through an inhaler, and are available in both short- and long-acting forms. Other drugs called anti-cholinergics are sometimes prescribed, especially for babies, but they take longer to work than ß-2 relievers and are not effective for everyone.

conventional treatment

RIGHT: Medication to relieve the symptoms of an asthma attack is usually presented in the form of an inhaler.

FAR RIGHT: It takes time and practice to learn to use an inhaler correctly, especially for a child, but it is vitally important.

SHORT-ACTING ß-2 RELIEVERS

Some doctors prefer to prescribe this treatment on its own for people whose asthma is mild, to be used only when they have an attack. However, because this approach can mask underlying inflammation and damage to the airways, the trend is towards prescribing small daily doses of preventive treatment while recommending that relievers are only used when absolutely necessary. ß-2 relievers work by stimulating the airways to expand and they can relieve symptoms such as shortness of breath, wheezing and tightness in the chest almost instantly. Normally, the effect lasts for about four hours. The problem with them is that they do nothing to halt the inflammation that is causing the symptoms and, if used too often, your airways eventually stop responding to them.

Too frequent use may also heighten the impact of the allergic response on the airways, so they then tend to narrow even when the level of allergens is relatively low. ß-2 relievers are a valuable part of asthma treatment, but it is important to use them in the right way. You should go back to your doctor if you find you are needing to use your inhaler more than once a day, to discuss adding (or increasing the dose of) preventive medication to your treatment regime. The exception to this rule is if you are having symptoms of a severe asthma attack, when you can take up to 30 puffs from your reliever while waiting for an ambulance or doctor to arrive.

LONG-ACTING ß-2 RELIEVERS

Some people whose attacks are not relieved by short-acting relievers or who are frequently troubled by symptoms during the night may do better with this form of inhaler. The drugs work in much the same way, although they take around 5–10 minutes to start working, and are then effective for around 10 hours. However, they are taken not only after an attack, but regularly twice a day. They are a better option for people who would otherwise need to use their short-acting relievers more than once a day, although they may also lose their effectiveness over a period of time.

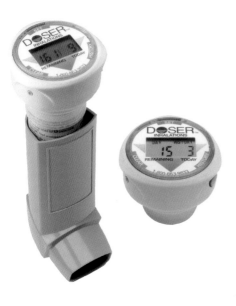

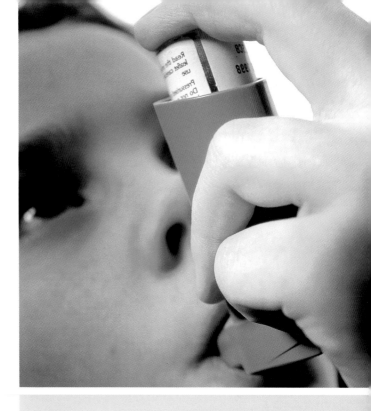

ANTI-CHOLINERGIC DRUGS

These drugs are designed to help the airways to resist narrowing through their effect on the nerves that control muscle tone. They take effect relatively slowly compared to ß-2 relievers – on average in about an hour – but remain effective for up to six hours. They are useful for young children, many of whom do not respond well to ß-2 relievers, and may work well for other asthma sufferers who have complications such as bronchitis, which mean they suffer from over-production of mucus. Anti-cholinergics may be prescribed instead of, or sometimes as well as, ß-2 relievers; the combination can be the right choice for some people whose asthma symptoms are otherwise difficult to control.

using an inhaler correctly

Initially, your doctor or asthma nurse should teach you how to use your inhaler properly, and let you practise while they watch to make sure you have mastered the technique. Don't be embarrassed if you find it difficult at first, and if you just cannot get the hang of using it after a while, ask if you can try a different kind. It is important to get this right; research has shown that using inhalers incorrectly is very common and can drastically reduce the amount of medication that reaches your lungs. There are basically three different types of inhaler: ordinary aerosol or puffer inhalers, aerosols that release the drug as you breathe in and dry-powder inhalers. There are several different models and designs within each of these categories, and all have potential advantages and disadvantages. The secret is to experiment for as long as necessary to find the one that suits you best. Anyone who finds all of them equally impossible may find taking their medication far easier if they use an aerosol inhaler together with a spacer (see page 38).

useful aids to treatment

Alongside the medication already mentioned, there are a number of aids that can be used to help take it more easily and more effectively. For some people, especially children, inhalers may prove to be too difficult to use. If this is the case, a spacer or, in some instances, a nebulizer may be recommended by your doctor as a means of delivering the necessary medication in a manageable form.

conventional
treatment

SPACERS

Young children (and adults who find inhalers difficult to use properly) may find it easier to take their asthma medication using a device called a spacer. Using one means you don't have to worry about coordinating breathing in and releasing the dose of the drug, nor do you have to be able to breathe in hard and deeply, which can be a problem if you're having an asthma attack. However, a spacer can only be used in conjunction with an aerosol inhaler; they don't work with the more modern dry-powder type.

Spacers come in a variety of shapes, sizes and materials, but they all do the same job. They look rather like small balloons with two holes. You spray the medicine from the inhaler through one hole and breathe it in through the other, which has a valve to prevent the vapour escaping. You can buy special spacers designed to be easier for young children to use – they include a mask to fit over the nose and mouth rather than a mouthpiece. It isn't necessary to take deep breaths to inhale the medication, so some parents prefer to fit the mask while the child is asleep if he or she finds taking medication difficult or distressing. Even if you normally have no problems using your inhaler, you may find it useful to have a spacer to enable you to take your reliever medication more easily during an asthma attack that leaves you short of breath. Check with the pharmacist when buying one to be sure that it is compatible with your particular type of inhaler.

NEBULIZERS

Anyone who has had treatment for a severe asthma attack in hospital or at the doctor's surgery will probably be familiar with these gadgets. They are also sometimes recommended for babies as it may be difficult for them to take their medication in any other way. They are used to deliver a relatively high concentration of reliever medication to the lungs in a relatively short period of time, but the majority of people with asthma don't need to consider getting one to use at home. A few people for whom high doses of drugs are the only way to control their symptoms may be advised by their doctor to use one on a regular basis and those who are unable to use inhalers may find a nebulizer is the best solution. However, the fact that they are designed to deliver a relatively high dose of drug with each treatment rules out their use on a daily basis for most people because of the increased risks of side effects (see page 34).

If you are one of those who are recommended by your doctor to keep a nebulizer for home use, you will be advised about which type would be most suitable and how to use and maintain it correctly.

RIGHT: A minority of people with asthma may need to take their medication through a nebulizer regularly.

an improvised spacer

If you or your child should have an asthma attack when you don't have a spacer on hand, you can use a paper bag or a plastic cup to make an emergency substitute, provided you have an aerosol reliever inhaler. Simply make an X-shaped cut in the base of a smooth plastic cup or a paper bag, though which you can insert the nozzle of the inhaler. You can place the cup or the open end of the bag over your mouth, spray the medication into the space from the other end, and breathe it in.

RIGHT: An improvized spacer can make it easier for someone having an asthma attack to inhale their reliever medication.

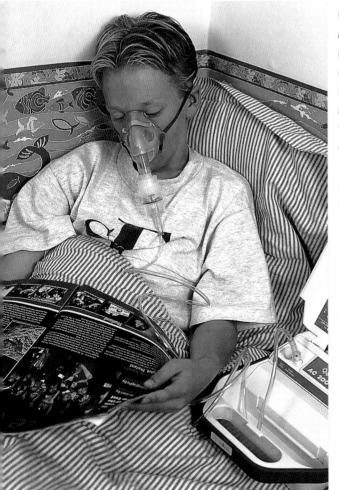

PEAK FLOW METERS

Unless your asthma is very mild, you will probably be advised by your doctor or asthma nurse to use a peak flow meter to monitor the state of your airways. When they are narrowed, the speed at which you can exhale air from your lungs will drop, and this could indicate either that your asthma is not being adequately controlled by your current treatment or that you could soon develop an attack if you don't take suitable action.

It is normal for people with asthma to find that their morning check gives a lower reading than their evening one, but if the gap between the two increases or if the readings are consistently lower than your 'best' performance, you need to see your doctor to discuss possible reasons and what can be done to rectify the situation. Doing twice daily readings is a bit of a chore, but if you can make it as much a part of your daily routine as cleaning your teeth, it should help you to keep your asthma under better control and minimize its effect on your normal life.

treatment for hay fever and perennial rhinitis

As with all allergic illness, people who suffer from rhinitis, whether on a seasonal or year-round basis, will be encouraged by their doctors to try and identify the allergens that trigger their symptoms and to take whatever steps they can to avoid them as much as possible. For more about how to do this, see the next chapter, 'Helping Yourself', pages 42–51. With seasonal rhinitis (or hay fever) in particular, you are unlikely to succeed completely in avoiding the triggers unless your rhinitis is a response to allergens such as pets or house dust mites.

Even if total avoidance is impossible, there is much that can be done through drug treatments to minimize symptoms and make life more comfortable for people with hay fever, even in the pollen season. The other main objective is to attempt to suppress the immune response.

conventional treatment

ANTI-HISTAMINES

Many different anti-histamines can be bought over the counter at the pharmacist in tablet form without a prescription. A few of the older types can make you drowsy, making it unsafe to drive or operate machinery, but newer ones do not usually have this effect on most people, so they are preferable. If you are buying them for yourself, ask the pharmacist for advice. If you are seeking treatment for a child, it's best to consult a doctor as some anti-histamines may be best avoided. The tablets are intended to counteract the release of histamines by mast cells during an allergic reaction, so preventing most of the symptoms. They work better for some individuals than others, and you may need to experiment with more than one brand before finding the one that suits you best. In any case, even if they are reasonably successful, you may need to use them in conjunction with some of the other medications listed here to get the optimum benefit.

You can also buy anti-histamine nose sprays which can help with a runny nose but don't usually relieve sore or watery eyes very much. As a rule, anti-histamines in general may be more use for people with seasonal rather than all-year symptoms of rhinitis.

DECONGESTANTS

Nose drops or sprays can give quick relief when your nose is uncomfortably blocked, but you should only use this form of treatment for short periods at a time. If you continue using them regularly for longer than about a fortnight, your nose will become dependent on their effectiveness. Once you stop using them you will experience what's called a 'rebound effect' and your blocked nose will be worse than ever. As a result, it is best to keep them for specific occasions – such as exams or an important celebration – when you want to feel as well as possible.

hyposensitization

A small minority of people with seasonal rhinitis whose symptoms are severe and who don't respond to any other treatment may be considered for this procedure. It has to be done by experts in a hospital because of the risk of triggering major side effects, especially anaphylactic shock (see page 30). It involves regular monthly injections of a solution containing your particular allergen until your immune system stops reacting to it (or them) so strongly. This may take up to three years, so it is not a treatment to be undertaken lightly.

RIGHT: Hay fever sufferers may not be able to avoid altogether the pollens to which they are sensitive.

SODIUM CROMOGLYCATE

This drug has few or no side effects and is frequently recommended for people who suffer from rhinitis symptoms all year round. It is designed to stop the mast cells releasing histamine and other chemicals that cause the symptoms. A nasal spray can be used up to four times a day, if needed. Eye drops are also available to soothe sore, watering eyes and itchy eyelids and, unlike the nasal sprays, are very effective for most people. If the nasal sprays don't seem to improve your condition, you may need to try some other form of treatment.

STEROIDS

Nasal sprays or drops containing corticosteroids (not the anabolic steroids sometimes misused by sports people) can be a very effective treatment for both nasal and eye symptoms. Because of the way the drug is delivered, very little gets beyond the target area, and in any case, they contain only a small amount of the drug, so you are very unlikely to get any side effects at all. Some types can be bought over the counter while others are only available on prescription, so if your hay fever is causing you real problems, it is worth asking your doctor's advice about what sort would be best for you.

Short courses of steroid tablets lasting for a week or two may be prescribed occasionally if your symptoms are severe and you need to be on top form for some particular event. However, the risk of side effects is such that these drugs are never given lightly, and if you can manage with other forms of treatment it is better to do so.

Fortunately, there is a lot that anyone with symptoms caused by an allergic reaction can do to help themselves, and such steps can make an enormous difference. **The first priority is to identify the allergens that are causing the symptoms, and the second, to take steps to avoid them as far as possible**. Both these tasks can involve a considerable amount of time and effort for some people, but it really is worthwhile because the benefits can be so great.

Potential allergens for asthma sufferers include house dust mite droppings, animal hair, moulds, industrial and household chemicals and, for a minority of people, certain foods, additives and medications. You also need to consider what other substances may make the symptoms worse, including cigarette smoke and other air pollutants. **With hay fever, symptoms are always caused by pollen or mould spores**, and you can usually make an educated guess as to which is responsible by the timing of your symptoms. You may also need to think about foods.

But as well as paying attention to allergens, **other lifestyle changes are worth trying, particularly for asthma sufferers. These can help to reduce the frequency and severity of attacks for some people**.

identifying and avoiding triggers

In many instances, it will be a relatively straightforward task to identify the allergen that is responsible for your symptoms, as with a pet allergy or hay fever caused by pollen, for example. Where you have some inkling of the cause but are not certain, it is worth keeping a detailed diary, recording when the symptoms come on, with details of your environment over the previous few hours, whether you were in contact with a pet, in a very dusty or damp building, what you ate and drank, and so on. If none of this sheds a clear light, you may need to have skin prick testing and/or blood tests (see page 21) to try to pin down the cause.

For people with asthma, potential allergens may include not only the commoner ones such as the droppings of house dust mites, animal hair and dander, moulds and industrial and household chemicals, but also, for a minority of people, certain foods or additives and particular medications. You may also need to consider what other substances may set off or exacerbate your symptoms, even though you are not, strictly speaking, allergic to them. These include cigarette smoke, ozone and other pollutants in the air, fumes and smells and, possibly, a wider range of foods and additives.

Some of the same substances, especially the droppings of house dust mites, pet material and moulds, may be responsible for the symptoms of

TAKE PRECAUTIONS

Many of the measures outlined on these pages will actually release pet allergens or mite droppings into the atmosphere while the work is being done, so it is preferable for the person suffering from asthma to get someone else to do these tasks if at all possible, and to keep a child with asthma out of the house for a few hours until the allergen levels have subsided.

HOUSE DUST MITES

These are by far the most common allergens as far as asthma is concerned and are also often responsible for triggering the symptoms of seasonal allergic rhinitis. It is in fact the droppings of these minuscule creatures that do the damage, and they are present in their millions throughout soft furnishings, curtains and bedding, even in the cleanest and most hygienic of homes. While reducing their numbers significantly is likely to involve a great deal of effort and some expense, the effect on symptoms can often be dramatic.

Concentrating on the bedroom is likely to have the most immediate effect. The aim is to kill existing mites and make the environment less comfortable for them to expand in numbers again. If you can, it is worth buying a new mattress and bedding as well as an anti-mite cover for the mattress, pillows and duvet. Recent research shows that pillows and duvets filled with synthetic material are not less allergenic than feather-filled ones, as was once thought.

Take measures to improve ventilation and reduce humidity in the home, and particularly in the bedroom; dry air discourages mites. Replacing carpets with non-textile floor coverings will help, otherwise vacuum carpets regularly and thoroughly either with a cleaner designed to reduce allergens or one with a filter fitted to the exhaust. Damp-dusting of surfaces should be done several times a week and all fabric items, including clothes and children's soft toys, should be washed at a high temperature (or dry-cleaned) frequently. Use similar measures in the sitting room as far as possible, washing curtains and loose covers at a high temperature and eliminating dust as much as possible. You can also buy aerosol sprays designed for use on upholstery which help to inactivate allergens. If you can afford to invest in a powerful dehumidifier, this will reduce moisture levels and discourage mites.

seasonal rhinitis. And again, there are other things that may make these symptoms worse, even though they are not actually allergens as far as you're concerned.

With hay fever, the culprit is always pollen of some kind or mould spores, and you can make an educated guess as to which group is responsible in your case by the timing of your symptoms. Pollens appear in the air at different times of the year depending on the source: the progression goes from trees to grasses to mould, from mid-spring through to early autumn. However, there is some overlap, and some people are sensitive to more than one kind, so you may need skin prick tests (see page 21) to identify the specific culprits if straightforward detection methods don't work. You may also need to think about foods. Depending on your particular allergy, you may experience what's called 'cross-reaction' to certain foods or ingredients (see page 67).

Both asthma and hay fever can also be made worse by irritants, and an important culprit seems to be the bright yellow blooms of oil seed rape. It is probable that it is not the pollen from this crop that causes problems but other chemicals which it releases into the air.

Some of the most common allergens are listed below, along with suggestions as to how you might reduce your contact with them.

aspirin and beta-blockers

A small proportion of people with asthma (estimated at 5–10 per cent) develop a sensitivity to aspirin-type drugs, including ibuprofen and non-steroidal anti-inflammatory drugs which are used to treat arthritis. This is most likely to happen if you have the small, harmless growths in your nose called polyps. The result may be an asthma attack, possibly combined with other symptoms such as a runny nose and red eyes, and feeling generally unwell. You should seek urgent medical help if this type of reaction develops, and take care to avoid taking aspirin-type medicines in future. People with asthma should never be prescribed beta-blockers – drugs used to treat some heart and circulatory problems – because they cause the airways to narrow and so may provoke a serious attack.

PETS

Unfortunately, any family in which someone is allergic to cats or dogs really must face the fact that keeping a pet is a very bad idea. However thoroughly you clean the house and bathe the animal and however stringent you are about keeping it out of the bedroom, for example, allergens will inevitably spread around the home and continue to trigger symptoms. What's more, the problem does not disappear even after you have steeled yourself to give your pet away – you will need to get rid of residues of allergens by washing all soft furnishings, bedding and any other fabric that may be contaminated. You will also need to vacuum repeatedly, preferably with an anti-allergen cleaner, and damp-dust all surfaces regularly for several weeks. Opening doors and windows to air all the rooms as thoroughly as possible will help to disperse allergens stirred up by all this activity.

MOULDS

Mould spores can trigger the allergic response in susceptible people, causing either asthma or perennial rhinitis symptoms. The key to reducing their presence in the home is to get rid of as much moisture and damp as you can, particularly in the bathroom and kitchen where it is a particular problem. Depending on where you live, this may necessitate dealing with problems such as rising damp and/or being scrupulous about cleaning off any signs of mould promptly and regularly. Installing extractor fans and a powerful dehumidifier are worthwhile if you can afford it, and train everyone to avoid anything that could increase overall moisture levels – leaving washing or damp towels to dry in the bathroom, for example.

helping yourself

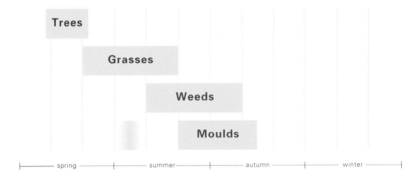

Trees			
	Grasses		
		Weeds	
		Moulds	
spring	summer	autumn	winter

pollen timetable

Trees Tree pollen is present for up to six weeks from early spring; the main culprits are likely to be hazel, plane, oak, elm, ash and birch.

Grasses Grass pollens are around from late spring until mid-summer; the main culprits include the wild meadow grasses rather than those planted by farmers for grazing such as rye grass.

Weeds Weed pollens are present from mid-summer to early autumn; docks, nettles, plantains, mugwort and, in the USA but not yet in the UK, ragweed may be responsible for symptoms.

Moulds Mould spores can cause symptoms from late summer to mid-autumn; however, one type called *Cladosporum herbarum* can appear as soon as early summer.

POLLEN

The fact that hay fever symptoms are most likely to be triggered by airborne grains of pollen makes it more difficult to avoid these allergens than those that are concentrated in the home, such as house dust mites. Nevertheless, by identifying which type of pollen causes you problems, and taking some sensible precautions to minimize your exposure to high levels of them during their peak season, you can do quite a lot to reduce their effects.

You can get a general idea of what type of pollen you are allergic to by taking note of the time of year when your symptoms begin (see the 'pollen timetable' above).

WHY POLLEN LEVELS FLUCTUATE

Although different plants release their pollen at slightly different times of the day, in general, concentrations are likely to peak in the early morning and early evening. But other factors can influence this pattern. The second peak often occurs a couple of hours earlier in the countryside than in towns and cities, and if there is little wind, there may be another rise soon after midnight. As a rule, the pollen count drops when it rains, especially if this happens early in the day, but thunderstorms can actually cause it to rise. High levels of humidity which occur just before a storm breaks cause pollen grains to burst and may also result in a rise in the levels of some types of mould spores. Pollen that is carried upwards into the atmosphere on warm mornings may be dispersed if it is very windy, causing fewer problems in the early evening, and counts are often lower on the coast, especially if there is a wind blowing off the sea.

In theory, you can find out the likely pollen count for any given day from the figures available through radio, television and telephone information lines, and plan your outdoor activities accordingly. This can certainly be useful, but bear in mind that predicting the count is not yet an exact science, and in any case, the count is likely to vary depending on local conditions and unexpected changes in the weather.

self-protection measures against pollen

→ Avoid being outside more than is necessary during the morning and evening pollen peaks, and when the count is high.

→ If you're staying indoors to minimize your exposure, remember to close all the windows and doors, especially in your bedroom at night, and train others in the family to cooperate.

→ If you're not a spectacle wearer, wear sunglasses out of doors during the day to protect your eyes from pollen grains.

→ Don't mow lawns yourself and stay inside with windows closed while it's being done.

→ When travelling by car, keep the windows closed, especially on motorways. Many new cars come with built-in pollen filters, and you can get one fitted to your existing car if necessary.

→ Apply a small amount of petroleum jelly to the inside of each nostril to attract pollen grains and so reduce the number that travel beyond your nose.

→ Shower, wash your hair and change your clothes when you come in from a pollen-laden atmosphere, especially in the early evening.

→ Don't dry washing outdoors in the pollen season.

→ Frequent damp-dusting, vacuuming daily (if possible with a cleaner incorporating a filter) and blocking any external ventilators and obvious draughts may all help to reduce the level of pollen inside your home.

→ Cats and dogs can carry pollen in their coats into the home, so, if at all possible, keep them outside during the pollen season. Bathing them regularly will help to get rid of the deposits, although your cat is unlikely to be cooperative.

→ If you're planning to move home, consider the possibility of living by the sea and/or at a relatively high altitude where pollen levels are lowest, and well away from meadows and 'set aside' land where they're likely to be high.

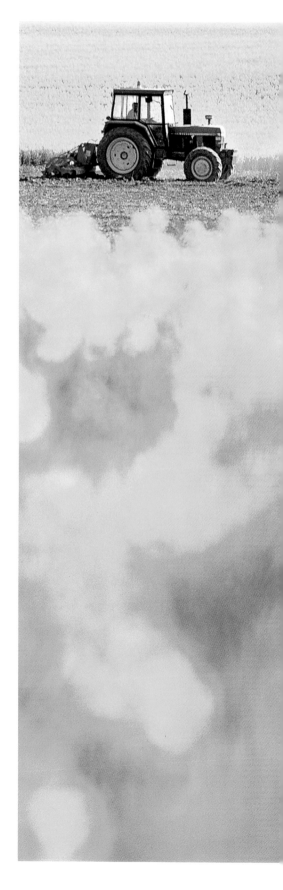

RIGHT: Pollen levels may peak earlier in the countryside than in towns.

helping
yourself

keeping your cool

Stress and heightened emotion do have an effect on people with allergy-related illness, but this is not to say that illnesses such as asthma and hay fever have a psychological cause. There is no evidence at all that this is the case, and the fact that you have one of these illnesses says nothing about your emotional or mental health one way or the other. However, it would be surprising if having one of these unpleasant and, in the case of asthma, potentially life-threatening conditions did not cause some of the individuals concerned to become anxious or depressed at times.

There is also good evidence that sudden or severe stress can some-times trigger the symptoms of asthma and even of hay fever, and part of the explanation lies in the close connection between the responses of the nervous system and physiological changes elsewhere in the body which are not fully understood. For example, it is possible that a reaction in the nerves that connect to the mast cells can trigger the cells to release the chain of chemicals which sets off the allergic reaction. Other interrelation-ships between stress and symptoms are better understood: everyone has experienced feelings of breathlessness when frightened or after a shock, and these effects can be magnified in people with asthma, causing their airways to narrow. Both sudden and chronic (or long-term) stress can have an effect on the airways, as can other strong emotions, even some pleasurable ones in certain instances.

RIGHT: If you are allergic to cats, your symptoms may be triggered by just seeing one.

ABOVE: Try not to let your anxiety about her asthma communicate itself to your child and avoid becoming over-protective.

caring for a child with asthma

It is hardly surprising that many parents worry about looking after a young child with asthma, and don't feel confident in their own ability to protect him or her from a serious attack. It can become even worse as the child gets older and tries to become more independent, even perhaps becoming reluctant to take regular medication or avoid situations that might trigger an attack. There is no one easy way to deal with all these worries, but having a sound understanding of your child's illness and its treatment, including what to do in an emergency, is a sound beginning. It is important that you try not to let your own anxiety well over on to your child, but encourage him or her in the belief that you can tackle the illness together. You may need to make a supreme effort to avoid becoming overprotective, and to allow your child to live as normal a life as possible, despite your fears. Don't be reluctant to seek help if you are finding the strain too much – talk to your doctor, a counsellor or other parents who have faced a similar situation – to help you build coping strategies.

Experiments have shown that if experience has taught you that your symptoms are usually provoked by walking through a grassy field or making close contact with a cat, for example, you may well react to the sight of these stimuli even if you are not actually breathing in grass pollen or cat dander.

One of the main reasons why it is important to know precisely what to do when you feel an asthma attack beginning (see page 26) is to help you to remain calm and avoid panicking. Fear and anxiety may be perfectly understandable reactions to the need to struggle for breath, but they are likely to make it more difficult to cope and take the correct action.

Whether you have an allergic illness or not, finding strategies both to reduce the overall levels of stress in your life and to manage it when you can't avoid it entirely will help to improve your general health and sense of well-being. Many of the complementary therapies described in the next chapter can be very effective in countering stress and tension, and those that focus on breathing may be particularly valuable for some people with asthma. For others, it may be more helpful to undertake a course of counselling or psychotherapy with the aim of developing a greater awareness of the underlying stress factors in your life and why you react to them in the way you do. While people with allergic illness are no more prone to psychological and emotional problems than anyone else, they are no more immune to them either, and for such individuals, tackling the deep-seated causes of anxiety and panic may be the most satisfactory approach.

Your doctor may be able to recommend a therapist or even offer such treatment in the surgery or health centre, but otherwise you may need to make your own arrangements. There are various organizations that train and register therapists who could give you names of people in your area, and friends and family may be able to make recommendations.

helping
yourself

exercise and breathing

Anyone who reads newspapers or magazines or watches television must be aware by now of the health benefits of regular exercise, and of the fact that the majority of people, including children, take too little. This applies just as much to people with allergic illness, including asthma, as it does to anyone else, although you will need to think a little more carefully about what you do and in what conditions.

Aerobic exercise, which increases the body's need for oxygen, strengthens the respiratory system and increases lung capacity as well as improving muscle tone and strength. However, many people with asthma have problems exercising outside unless it is relatively warm because breathing in cold air can trigger an attack. People who know that it is exercise as such that tends to bring on symptoms (those with exercise-induced asthma, or EIA) may find it helps to adjust their medication to enable them to participate without problems. Your doctor or asthma nurse may suggest taking an extra dose of your usual reliever or taking sodium cromoglycate as well as a steroid preventer to make symptoms less likely. If you have hay fever, it obviously doesn't make sense to do outdoor activities at the height of the pollen season, but there are plenty of indoor alternatives to choose from.

One of the most beneficial sports for people who are unfit or find other activities problematic is swimming, although heavy chlorination in some pools can irritate the airways in sensitive individuals. If you are unaccustomed to exercise, you can take it gently at first, and gradually increase the amount of effort you put in as your muscles build up strength and stamina. You might also want to consider gym, dancing, badminton or even martial arts, to name but a few readily available indoor activities, but the main priority is to find something you actually enjoy. Few people have the willpower to stick at something they hate doing, just because they know it's good for them.

HYPERVENTILATION

Evolution has arranged things so that when we feel anxious or under threat, our bodies make certain preparations to enable us to either run away or do battle with the enemy. This response is usually referred to as the 'fight or flight' mechanism. While this made sense in the world of primitive man, it is less use today when threats are more likely to be psychological than physical. One of the elements in our response to threats or anxieties is to breathe faster, using our upper chest muscles to take in more air. While this has few effects in the very short term, if you continue doing it, it will upset the natural balance of carbon dioxide in your body and the consequences can mimic or exacerbate the symptoms of asthma. Some people get into the habit of overbreathing (hyperventilating) most of the time, and many do it in the course of an asthma attack to try to increase their air intake. This can cause a wide range of symptoms including, oddly, feeling breathless, as well as a sense of panic and imminent doom. It may also subtly affect the symptoms of an asthma attack by increasing the amount of histamine released by the mast cells and the tendency of the airways to contract.

If you suspect that you have a tendency to overbreathe, you should consult your doctor who may, if appropriate, arrange for you to see a physiotherapist who can teach you how to overcome the habit. You may also benefit from a course of yoga or other disciplines such as t'ai chi (see page 54), in which controlled breathing is an important element.

ABOVE: Do not go cycling in the pollen season if you have hay fever.

BELOW: Swimming is good exercise for people with allergies, provided the water is not heavily chlorinated.

children and exercise

Several studies have shown that children in most Western countries are suffering the consequences of being physically inactive – obesity and the early signs of cardiovascular disease among them. Provided proper precautions are followed, there is no reason why a child with asthma should not join in most of the activities enjoyed by their schoolmates, and by doing so, they will benefit psychologically as well as physically. Having to remain on the sidelines in any kind of games can make a child feel socially excluded and 'different' from their friends, and may well have adverse effects on their social development and self-image. If your child's physical education teacher is not already well-informed about asthma (and many are), you should arrange to meet him or her and discuss any potential difficulties and how to handle them if necessary.

chapter 5

If you've never tried any form of complementary therapy before, you may be surprised at the **huge range of options available and the benefits they can offer to people with symptoms of allergic disease**. However, it is important to remember that these therapies are, in almost all cases, designed to supplement orthodox treatment and definitely not to replace it.

No complementary practitioner is in a position to offer you a cure and you should steer clear of anyone who even implies that this might be possible. Nevertheless, **complementary therapy can often do a lot to help relieve symptoms and, in particular, to influence important factors such as your psychological response to your condition and your ability to relax and to control your breathing**.

People with conditions that cannot be cured, and who inevitably have to follow the advice of doctors and other health professionals much of the time, often turn to complementary therapy because it **opens up the prospect of doing something to help themselves**. Most complementary practitioners lay stress on being an active partner in therapy, and this can help to empower you to influence your own well-being.

complementary
treatments

Partly at least because they can give each person more time, complementary practitioners are more inclined than orthodox physicians to adopt a holistic view: that is, they see you as a unique individual whose whole lifestyle is relevant to your treatment, and want to know a lot more about you than simply what symptoms you have. Only when they know this can they decide the best way to help you.

active approaches

Yoga, t'ai chi and the various martial arts all involve physical movement integrated with attention to breathing and elements of Eastern philosophy to a greater or lesser degree. Although they can be physically demanding, they generally don't require the bursts of sustained energy needed by runners or players of team games such as rugby. However, they do demand commitment and regular attendance at classes.

YOGA

Depending on which of the various schools of yoga your teacher subscribes to, the balance of the class may shift between postures (asanas), breathing exercises (pranayama) and meditation. One of the most encouraging features of yoga classes, especially for the unfit, is that any element of competition is firmly discouraged; the aim is to stay within your own limits, while gradually extending them.

Ideally, your teacher should have some knowledge of asthma and understand that your ability to perform deep breathing exercises may be limited to some extent. Postures that involve stretching and strengthening your back and breathing muscles and that expand your chest can help to dissipate tightness which has built up as a result of muscular tension. A good yoga teacher will place great emphasis on thorough relaxation, and in most classes you will spend a proportion of time learning how to do this properly. If you decide to practise what you have learned in class on your own at home, resist any temptation to concentrate on the postures at the expense of relaxation and breathing techniques as these are a vital part of the discipline. Provided that your yoga teacher is sensitive to potential problems and that you don't try to push yourself too far too fast, you may find that regular sessions help you to remain calm and may even mean you have fewer or less serious attacks.

T'AI CHI

Tourists in Hong Kong and China will almost certainly have seen local people performing the movements of t'ai chi in parks and open spaces everywhere, oblivious of the curious onlookers. The movements are slow and gentle, and look almost like freestyle ballet or mime, but they are believed to confer both mental and physical benefits on those who do them. As well as improving body flexibility and strength, the exercises are designed to eliminate muscular tension as well as improving the flow of 'chi' (defined as the life force or intrinsic energy) through the body.

In order to perform the slow sequences of movements properly, practitioners must focus totally on what they are doing and on regular, controlled breathing. Stillness is as important as movement itself, and the energy demands are not high, which makes t'ai chi a useful starting point for anyone who does not feel up to more vigorous exercise as well as for those who find it hard to master meditation and pure breathing exercises.

It takes patience to learn t'ai chi, but if it appeals to you, it is a good way to combine relaxation and easing muscular stress with gentle physical exercise.

RIGHT: Yoga combines elements of postures, breathing and meditation and encourages participants to avoid competing with one another.

BELOW: There is much more to Eastern martial arts than techniques of self-defence.

MARTIAL ARTS

Those who prefer something more active and strenuous may want to opt for classes in one of the martial arts such as judo or aikido. Although they may be seen by non-practitioners purely as systems of self-defence, these and related activities involve strict self discipline and elements of philosophy, which mean they have more in common with yoga than they do with boxing, for example. As you become adept at the art, you will certainly develop stronger muscles and become more flexible, but you will also learn to focus on your breathing and to be calm and in control at all times.

will they improve your asthma?

Any activity that tones and relaxes your muscles and reduces the effects of stress can only have positive consequences for your overall health and sense of well-being. The mental and spiritual components of these active approaches, which have their roots in Eastern philosophy and medicine, can be especially helpful to you if you have a tendency to anxiety and worry, in addition to their physical benefits. No one can say for certain that they will actually reduce your symptoms, but many people feel better as a result of practising the techniques on a regular basis.

relaxation

complementary
treatments

There is a lot more to relaxation than slumping on the sofa in front of the television. It encompasses both the physical and the psychological, and many people need to learn specific techniques to achieve it.

Stress and anxiety can lead to the build-up of knots of tension in the muscles, particularly around the neck, shoulders and abdomen, all of which can make breathing more difficult. If you suffer from constant low-level anxiety about an asthma attack, tension is more likely to build up and it will diminish your ability to cope well with any problems. In particular, the calmer you are able to remain if and when an attack does actually strike, the better you will manage and you may even be able to diminish its length or severity or even abort it altogether.

RELAXATION

One of the most popular relaxation techniques is to lie in a quiet room where you will not be disturbed, and work your way slowly through a well-defined sequence of muscular relaxation. You lie on your back with your hands loosely by your sides. Then, beginning at the toes, clench the muscles tightly for several seconds before relaxing them. You gradually work your way up the body – calves, knees, thighs, pelvis and so on, remembering to include hands and arms – until you reach your face. Pay particular attention to your shoulders, neck, jaw and facial muscles, taking as much time as you need and trying to concentrate on the exercise without letting your thoughts stray.

MEDITATION AND VISUALIZATION

If you wish, you can learn formal techniques of meditation at classes based on particular philosophies such as Zen, but it is also possible to develop the technique on your own at home. You need to select something on which to focus your mind – it might be a candle flame or a particular word or short phrase (or 'mantra') which you repeat silently and continuously to yourself. The object is to concentrate your attention exclusively on whatever you have chosen, trying to expel other thoughts and bring your attention constantly back to this focus whenever it begins to wander. You will probably find this difficult to achieve for more than a minute or two at first, but it does get easier with practice. If you find it impossible to concentrate on a flame or a mantra, you may like to buy one of the many readily available cassette tapes, often featuring a soothing voice or sounds, to help you clear your head.

Visualization is a similar technique, except that you choose a picture (either a real one or a mental image) which you associate with calm and peace and practise concentrating on this and the sensations it conjures up for you. Many people opt for a tranquil seascape but you should choose whatever works best for you.

RIGHT: Once you have mastered the technique, you can practise meditation or visualization anywhere, whenever you need to.

BELOW: Acupuncture has been used by physicians in China for centuries and is now becoming increasingly popular in other countries.

ACUPUNCTURE AND SHIATSU

Acupuncture is an ancient Chinese system of medicine which aims to promote health and heal sickness by applying fine needles to the skin at certain specified points. These are located on various invisible 'meridians' along which 'chi' – the life energy – is believed to flow and stimulating them is designed to restore the natural balance and harmony. It has been suggested by some Western scientists that acupuncture may in fact stimulate the production of chemicals called endorphins which have pain-relieving properties. It is possible that it may have some effect in preventing narrowing of the airways, but the only way to find out whether you can benefit from the treatment is to try it and see.

Shiatsu is a Japanese therapy based on principles similar to acupuncture, but instead of using needles the therapist manipulates the acupuncture points (or 'tsubos') by applying various different kinds of pressure with the fingers and thumbs.

As with most forms of complementary therapy, acupuncture and shiatsu practitioners tailor their treatment to the individual, which means that different points may be selected for treatment even though two individuals have the same condition and very similar symptoms.

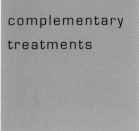

complementary
treatments

massage

We all instinctively rub an injury to stop it hurting, and the practice of using touch to heal pain and sickness is possibly the oldest form of medicine. From this basic premise, massage treatment has developed in many forms in different cultures all over the world, but perhaps the most widely known in the West are those based on Swedish massage. Practitioners have a good knowledge of anatomy and use a range of strokes with varying levels of pressure, using a small quantity of massage oil to help the hands glide over the skin. When appropriate, they also use a technique known as mobilization – taking the limbs through their range of movement around a joint – to restore flexibility and mobility.

MASSAGE

Although massage therapists would make no specific claims as regards treating asthma and allergy-related conditions, their treatment has two potential benefits to offer. The first is that it is one of the best and easiest ways to achieve complete relaxation; people often have trouble staying awake by the end of a session, however wound-up they were when it began. Most people find it a pleasant and thoroughly enjoyable experience, and especially appreciate the sense of peace and calm that pervades the treatment room. For anyone who finds themself becoming stressed by having to cope with their condition as well as the demands of everyday life, regular massage sessions can be an excellent antidote.

Secondly, massage is a very effective means of eliminating tension from muscles and other soft tissue, especially in the upper body. This can be particularly beneficial for people who experience frequent asthma symptoms, as it helps to counteract the muscular tension which often builds up around the neck, shoulders, chest and abdomen.

Some massage therapists and practitioners who specialize in aromatherapy use essential oils, derived from plants, to enhance the effects of the treatment. They are believed to have therapeutic effects both through inhalation and direct absorption through the skin, and will be chosen according to the recipient's personal preferences as well as for their intrinsic qualities. However, although they are only ever used blended with neutral oils, such as vegetable oil, their scent can be very powerful, and some may irritate the airways of sensitive people. For this reason, they should only be used very cautiously, if at all, if you have asthma or rhinitis.

There are a host of other related therapies in which massage plays a part, some of them based on similar principles to Swedish massage; others are derived from traditional Oriental massage and work on concepts such as balancing the flow of life energy, or harmonizing the elements of 'yin' and 'yang', for example. Some are more easily available than others, but if you have a wide choice it may be best to begin with whatever style of therapy you feel most drawn to.

RIGHT: Massage and aromatherapy are both extremely effective ways of relieving muscular tension, especially in the neck, back and shoulders.

FAR RIGHT: Osteopaths and chiropractors use manipulation techniques to correct misalignments that are disrupting the body's natural balance and function.

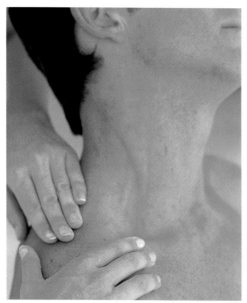

OSTEOPATHY AND CHIROPRACTIC

Osteopaths and chiropractors have considerable success in treating back pain for which conventional medicine often has little to offer. Although they use manual manipulation to work on the bones, joints, muscles and soft tissues, osteopaths aim to restore the body to its natural state of health which depends on a proper relationship between the structure and function of all its constituent parts. For example, if a particular bone is out of correct alignment, this can adversely affect not only the surrounding soft tissues but also how the nervous system works.

As far as asthma is concerned, treatment is likely to be concentrated on correcting skeletal misalignments in the upper torso and any resultant muscular tension and stiffness which have developed due to faulty breathing habits and excessive inflation of the lungs. Contrary to what many people believe, osteopathic manipulation often employs very gentle pressure and manipulation and is rarely if at all painful. Treatment is preceded by a very detailed study of the way you move, stand and sit, and the practitioner will pick up any poor posture or bad breathing habits and advise you how to correct them with exercises.

Chiropractors use many of the same techniques as osteopaths, but they tend to concentrate most on problems originating in the structure of the spine. Diagnosis may require X-rays and a thorough history of symptoms.

THE ALEXANDER TECHNIQUE

Originally devised to help actors who had problems with posture and breathing, the Alexander technique is less a therapy than a way of tuning in to your body and the way you stand, sit and move. The aim is to learn to lose the bad postural habits that almost everyone develops over time, in particular, the way you hold your head in relation to your spine, tensing muscles and restricting your breathing. Many people with asthma have found that a course of lessons in 'bodily re-education' has helped with their breathing and general sense of well-being.

At least initially, you should attend classes run by a qualified teacher to ensure that you are learning the technique correctly.

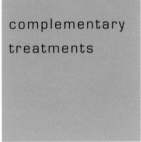

complementary
treatments

finding a
complementary therapist

Once you have made up your mind what kind of complementary therapy you would like to try, it's worth asking around to see whether anyone has any recommendations. Otherwise you could try the local health food shop or the notice board at your nearest leisure centre. Most therapists will be happy to arrange an initial meeting to discuss your condition and needs, and you should take the opportunity to check on their training and qualifications. It's also a good idea to ask what experience he or she has had of treating people with similar problems to yours before committing yourself to a course of treatment.

You also need to know how much a session will cost and how many you are likely to need over what period of time before you see any benefit. Take note of what you're told and bear it in mind when you begin your

HOMEOPATHY

Devised in the 19th century, homeopathic treatment works on the principle that 'like cures like'. This means giving a patient the remedies that would be expected to provoke the same symptoms from which they are suffering. Usually given in the form of small pills, remedies are prepared by diluting the original preparation (or tincture) of the active substance many times over using a technique called 'percussion' (or shaking) which is said to increase its potency many times. In their final form, the remedies contain no measurable trace of the original substance, which is the major reason why many people doubt that they can have any real physical effect. Nevertheless, homeopaths (some of whom are also orthodox physicians) and their many satisfied patients have no doubt that the right treatment can and does work.

When you first consult a homeopath, he or she will spend a great deal of time asking very detailed questions about your symptoms as well as other aspects of your life and try to learn something of your personality. The remedies eventually prescribed will be different for every individual, regardless of how similar their symptoms may be.

Many homeopaths will only agree to treat a person with asthma on a long-term basis. They will prescribe remedies appropriate to that individual's constitution –

their lifestyle and vulnerability to illness – as well as to prevent and alleviate attacks.

You can buy homeopathic remedies to treat yourself over the counter from many chemists, although you may prefer to consult a homeopathic pharmacist if you have never used this form of treatment before. Whether they work for you or not, homeopathic remedies will do no harm and have no known side effects.

treatment; there's no point in wasting your time or money if you are not seeing any results after a reasonable period of time.

Go no further with any therapist who suggests that his or her treatment can replace the medicines you normally take, especially if you have asthma. In any case, it's a good idea to let your doctor know what kind of treatment you are considering, even if you expect a hostile or sceptical reaction. Listen to what he or she says if they advise against a particular therapy as there may be a sound reason why it would not be the right thing for you.

If you find that you feel so much better following a course of treatment that you feel you could safely change your drug regime, talk to your doctor first and make any changes on a step-by-step basis rather than all at once.

ROYAL JELLY

If you are allergic to pollen, you should not use remedies such as royal jelly or propolis as these could make your symptoms worse or trigger a severe allergic reaction.

HERBAL MEDICINE

Many people are attracted to the idea of herbal medicine because they believe that remedies derived from plants are somehow more natural and therefore safer than the drugs prescribed by orthodox doctors. In fact, this is not necessarily the case at all, and some remedies may contain powerful active substances that could well have unpredicted side effects. Although many well-known conventional treatments, including aspirin, the heart drug digitalis as well as the anti-allergic medicine sodium cromoglycate, were derived originally from plants, herbal remedies have not been tested for safety or effectiveness in the same way as pharmaceutical drugs.

There are some herbal remedies that research suggests may have beneficial effects on the airways in people with asthma. However, rather than treat yourself, you would be well-advised to consult an experienced practitioner who has gone through extensive training and will be aware of the relative potential benefits and side effects of treatment.

LEFT: The range of herbal treatments that are now available over the counter is enormous, but there are no guarantees as to their effectiveness or freedom from side effects.

the food connection

If you are one of the many people who believe that your symptoms are sometimes triggered by food, you may have trouble convincing your doctors. The prevailing view among most asthma and allergy physicians is that true food allergy plays a significant part in only 2–3 per cent of people with asthma. With rhinitis, it is accepted that **some people with an allergy to particular pollens may also react to certain foods**.

The situation is complicated by the fact that certain foods and additives may cause symptoms because they act as irritants rather than causing a true allergic response. If your airways have become hypersensitized as a result of asthma, they may react to these irritants by narrowing, so triggering symptoms of an asthma attack. Whatever the mechanism, **it is clear that symptoms of asthma and rhinitis can be triggered by foods in some people**, although this may or may not involve a true allergic reaction. An allergic response often includes non-respiratory symptoms such as a rash, swelling around the mouth and lips and wheezing, making it easier to identify, at least. But very often it is more difficult to be sure whether foods and which ones may be causing or worsening symptoms of asthma or rhinitis because the effect may take several hours to develop.

the food
connection

are you allergic?

If you or your child have ever experienced any symptoms of a true food allergy, including swelling of the mouth and lips and an immediate skin reaction, it is essential that you discuss the situation with your doctor. There is a serious risk that your symptoms will be more severe next time you eat the same food or will gradually get worse with every future encounter with it, and could ultimately result in the life-threatening ana-phylactic shock (see page 30). This certainly doesn't happen to everyone, but it is better not to take any chances.

True food allergy can often be diagnosed through the use of skin prick and/or blood tests (see page 21) if necessary, although sometimes the culprit is obvious, especially if it is one of the common allergens such as peanuts. Tests may not be needed either if you can make a direct connec-tion between eating a particular food and the rapid onset of symptoms, but this isn't always the case. Sometimes the offending food may be present but disguised in a meal with many different ingredients. Diagnosis becomes even more problematic if there is a delay of several hours or more between consuming the culprit food and the start of your symptoms. In this situation, it may help to keep a detailed diary over a period of a few weeks in which you record exactly what you have eaten or drunk and when, and the timing and nature of your symptoms.

Although the various allergy tests can often identify whether you are experiencing a true allergic reaction – and to what – they are not totally reliable. In any case, they tend to be less effective at picking up allergies to specific foods or ingredients than at identifying other types of allergens such as pollen or house dust mites. Both false-negative and false-positive results can occur. For example, you may still develop allergic symptoms to a particular food or certain ingredients even though your test results are negative. Conversely, some people who show a positive response to testing do not actually develop allergic symptoms when they consume the allergen.

If these tests are inconclusive or not thought to be appropriate for some reason, it may be necessary when symptoms are causing real problems to resort to an elimination diet. This means eating a very limited range of foods that rarely or never cause allergic reactions, and gradually introducing suspect foods to test for a reaction. It is a long and rather tedious process and, ideally, should be done under the guidance of an allergy specialist or dietician, because of the need to ensure that you do not become malnourished or make mistakes that undermine the reliability of any conclusions.

However, if you are unable to get the right kind of help, you can try a modified elimination-type diet by yourself. It is possible to do so provided you are sensible and sufficiently motivated. For more information on how to go about this safely, see page 70.

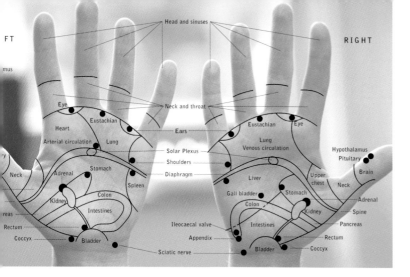

Head and sinuses

FT   RIGHT

tests to avoid

As yet there is no test or investigation, other than a properly managed elimination diet, that can diagnose food allergy or intolerance with complete reliability. This is naturally frustrating for patients and doctors alike, so it is not surprising that many people with suspected but unconfirmed food-related symptoms are tempted by individuals or organizations offering quick and easy answers. There are a number of different so-called diagnostic tests on offer, all of which have to be paid for. They range from blood tests, such as the cytotoxic test, hair analysis and one called the Vega test which uses acupressure points on the fingers, to others that supposedly measure energy flow or muscle resistance using electronic devices of various kinds. There are even some that don't require the presence of the patient or any sample from their body – the practitioner can apparently diagnose the problem simply by talking to them on the telephone or just thinking about them!

Such tests may be offered in health food stores, in 'alternative' clinics and through mail-order advertisements in newspapers and magazines. Inevitably, such tests will sometimes come up with the right answer, if only because many people with allergies react to one of the commoner culprit foods such as dairy produce or wheat, for example, but they are more often likely to be completely wrong.

If you are concerned about symptoms that are food-related, you won't help yourself by opting for any of these supposed short cuts; you'll be none the wiser afterwards and may be considerably poorer. What's more, acting on the results could mean you are continuing to consume the genuine problem foods while taking a lot of trouble to avoid others that have no adverse effect on your health whatsoever.

TOP: Paying for tests which use alternative methods or offer a quick answer is a waste of money. Complementary treatments, such as reflexology and acupressure, can help symptoms, but won't be able to establish which foods you are allergic to.

ABOVE: Allergy tests in health food shops, by post or telephone are unreliable and cannot give an accurate diagnosis.

potential problem foods

TOP: Many fruits and vegetables can trigger allergic symptoms and people with hay fever may experience cross-reactions.

ABOVE: If you react to shellfish you may decide that it is easier to avoid it altogether than to try to pinpoint specific culprits.

COMMON TRIGGERS

In theory, virtually any food can cause an allergic reaction, but in practice, some are very much more likely to do so than others. The same is true of those that trigger unpleasant symptoms, even though you are not, strictly speaking, allergic to them. It's not usually possible to 'treat' the food concerned in any way to neutralize the potential allergen – cooking has no effect in most cases, for example. Although some people do actually dislike the foods to which they are allergic, many more like those particular foods very much and, in some cases, actually crave them and eat them as often as possible. If you do suspect that some of your symptoms may be the result of food allergy or intolerance but can't immediately pin down the culprits, you might start by suspecting your favourites – the foods or dishes you would hate to have to go without.

Foods to which people are most often allergic or intolerant are listed below, although remember that your particular bugbear may not be mentioned.

→ **Cows' milk** This may cause problems especially in babies and children, a minority of whom may develop symptoms because their digestive system lacks the enzyme necessary to digest milk protein. Anyone who has problems with cows' milk may also react in a similar way to goats' milk.

→ **Cereals** Wheat is probably the major culprit in this group, possibly because it is present in so many foods that are a common feature of our diet in Western countries.

→ **Eggs** Although it is the white part that is responsible for most symptoms, it is so easy for the yolk to be contaminated with tiny amounts of white that it is best to avoid eating eggs altogether.

→ **Fruit and vegetables** Allergic reaction is likely to be a problem primarily for people with pollen allergies which trigger asthma or hay fever symptoms (see 'cross-reactions', page 67).

→ **Nuts** As well as the potentially serious nut allergies mentioned on page 30, some people with pollen allergies may also react to walnuts and hazelnuts.

→ **Fish and shellfish** Although these are common allergens, with shellfish in particular likely to cause dramatic symptoms, it is a difficult area because many people who are affected by some varieties can tolerate others perfectly well.

→ **Yeast** Anyone who reacts to this will need to avoid any drink fermented with it – such as wine or beer – as well as a whole range of bakery foods such as bread and doughnuts, and yeast extracts.

FOOD ADDITIVES

People with allergic conditions may find that their attacks are triggered or made worse when they eat foods containing certain food additives, usually because they are acting as irritants rather than as allergens. The ones most likely to cause problems are:

→ **Sulphites** These are chemicals used as preservatives in many foods and also in brewing and wine-making. They give off minute quantities of sulphur gas which can irritate the lungs of sensitive people, but because they are present in so many foods and drinks, it is worth keeping a careful symptom diary to establish whether they affect you, as avoiding them isn't easy. Packaged foods must list sulphites on their ingredients lists, but you also need to be wary of prepared salads, dried apricots and French fries in restaurants and takeaways.

→ **Tartrazine** This is a yellow colouring that is still added to some food and drink, though its use is less widespread than it once was because it has been linked with hyperactivity in children. It is most likely to cause problems for people who also react badly to aspirin.

→ **MSG** Otherwise known as monosodium glutamate, this is a flavour enhancer widely used in Chinese restaurant and takeaway meals, and also in prepared foods such as soups and some stock cubes.

CROSS-REACTIONS

A minority of people who are allergic to particular pollens may sometimes experience a reaction to certain foods. This may be because the foods in question are derived from plants in the same family as that which produces the pollen concerned, or because they share certain allergens. The most widely recognized cross-reaction is between birch pollen allergy and apples, and sometimes also other fruits including pears, peaches, apricots and nectarines. Cooking the fruit solves the problem. People who are allergic to latex may also be allergic to tropical fruits, including avocados; this must be taken seriously as it can result in a severe allergic reaction.

histamine

As we saw in Chapter 2, symptoms of asthma and rhinitis are triggered in part by the release of histamine by the mast cells during an allergic reaction. Consuming any food or drink that contains this substance can make an attack worse for people who are sensitive to it. If you do react in this way, you will need to steer clear of anything containing it; likely culprits include very mature or ripe cheeses, tuna, salami-style sausage and sometimes wine.

TOP: Physical activity combined with a healthy diet is the best way to shed excess weight.

other dietary factors

WEIGHT

If you know you are carrying too much weight for your height and bone structure, you may not be entirely surprised to learn that obesity can make a condition such as asthma worse. Most overweight people have read enough and seen enough on television about the adverse affects a burden of body fat can have on their health in general, increasing the risk of developing heart disease, one kind of diabetes and much else besides. Unfortunately, it can also make you more prone to develop asthma if you don't already have it.

Being seriously overweight puts a strain on all the organs of your body, and can make it more difficult for the lungs to expand properly. Unfortunately, carrying extra weight also increases your muscles' demand for oxygen – think how breathless you become carrying a heavy suitcase up a long flight of stairs, for example. If your lungs are already struggling or not working at maximum capacity, the additional burden imposed on them by obesity can aggravate the symptoms.

Despite the profusion of 'quick fix' slimming diets around, there is really only one sensible way to lose weight and that is to consume fewer calories than you burn. In recent years, the emphasis among dieticians has shifted from drastic reductions in calorie intake to an increase in exercise, in part because physical activity brings other health benefits besides weight loss. Following a healthy diet that is high in fruit, vegetables and complex carbohydrates, and low in sugar, fat and alcohol, will be sufficient to begin shifting the pounds for most people, assuming they go for modest rather than vast portions. However, combining this sort of diet with regular exercise will have a much bigger impact. Not only will you burn up calories by increasing your activity levels, you will also replace fat with muscle, which burns more calories.

If you avoid exercise because you know it triggers your asthma attacks, you need to plan your programme carefully and consult your doctor or asthma nurse about adjusting your medication to make symptoms less likely (see page 50).

HEARTBURN

Heartburn is a type of indigestion that can be very uncomfortable or even painful at times. The main symptom is often a burning sensation in the middle of the chest together with small quantities of the contents of your stomach coming back up into your throat and mouth, causing an unpleasant acidic taste. You may find you are prone to choke on your food and to feel 'windy' and bloated after a meal.

The symptoms are the result of partially digested food coming back up the 'food pipe' (or oesophagus) because the valve at the top of your stomach which is supposed to stop this happening isn't working properly. Doctors call this condition gastro-intestinal reflux, and people with asthma seem to be more susceptible to it. Apart from being unpleasant in itself, heartburn can trigger an asthma attack, usually because the irritated nerves in the oesophagus trigger a narrowing of the airways. If you happen to inhale any tiny particles of the regurgitated substances in your mouth, these may ultimately reach the airways themselves and cause irritation.

There are various medications available both on prescription and over the counter from a pharmacy to treat the condition, but if it is causing you real problems, you should see your doctor.

You can also help yourself by taking a few common-sense precautions against heartburn.

→ **Avoid eating your last meal late in the evening.**

→ **Steer clear of very spicy, fatty or acidic foods, or anything that you know triggers your symptoms.**

→ **Don't wear tight belts or clothes that constrict you around the waist.**

→ **Raise the head of your bed a little; a couple of telephone directories under the top legs will do the trick.**

→ **Sit comfortably after a meal and try to avoid bending down for an hour or so after you've eaten.**

A few people may experience asthma attacks that are actually triggered by this type of indigestion, even though they have no classic heartburn symptoms. You should see your doctor if you notice that your attacks often follow soon after eating a meal.

elimination and low-allergen diets

The aim of these limited diets is to identify and ultimately to avoid foods that are causing or aggravating your symptoms, particularly when they are rather ill-defined and come on some time after you have eaten. If you have ever had any of the symptoms that suggest you could have a specific food allergy of the type that causes the symptoms listed on page 30, you should never attempt this approach without medical supervision. There is a risk of provoking a full-scale reaction, which could result in anaphylactic shock when you reintroduce the food to which you are allergic. Because it involves restricting the range of foods eaten in the first stage, extreme caution is also needed with children who may not be able to get all the vital nutrients and energy they need while they are growing and developing from a limited diet. Even as an adult, you should seek advice from your doctor if you are planning to try this kind of diet, and it

your food and symptom diary

Around two weeks before you would be starting the diet if you go ahead, note down every single thing you eat or drink, with the time you did so. Note down too exactly how you are feeling at various points during the day and whether you have any asthma or rhinitis symptoms. Should your symptoms get worse or begin at any stage, write this in your diary, together with the time and what you are feeling. Don't forget to keep a record of any other symptoms, such as digestive upset, as well.

If you have asthma and normally use a peak flow meter, make a special effort to measure and record your peak flow every morning and evening, even if you don't do so on a daily basis normally. If you need to increase your dose of medication at any point, write down the details. Finally, don't forget to include any other factors that might have a bearing on your symptoms, such as unexpected bursts of physical activity, spending time in a very smoky room or a major emotional upset.

If studying your record after two weeks doesn't seem to shed any light on your situation, continue for another couple of weeks. If there is still no obvious pattern, think again about whether it is worthwhile embarking on a diet. It may be that your symptoms are not in fact diet-related, or if they are, you are reacting to so many different things that the puzzle is probably too complex for you to solve without professional help.

would be the best course of action if he or she could arrange for you to do so under the guidance of a dietician.

The point of embarking on a limited diet is to eventually allow you to eat a healthy diet of foods you enjoy while steering clear of those items that cause problems. It is important to be as confident as you can that food is a factor in your symptoms, otherwise you will be making life unnecessarily difficult for yourself, possibly missing out on meals you enjoy without gaining any health benefits to make all the effort worthwhile. Unless you already have a very strong suspicion as to the culprit foods, it is worth keeping a diary to see whether there is any pattern. Do your symptoms seem to be connected to what you eat and drink or not? If so, does the record suggest any likely suspects? Don't forget to check the nutritional labels of any prepared foods carefully, noting particularly what additives they contain. You will find some of those that are known to trigger symptoms in sensitive people listed on page 67. You should also look out for a few items that may be derived from a possible problem food, such as whey or casein which come from milk.

ABOVE: Ideally, you should ask your doctor to refer you to a dietician who can guide you through an elimination diet.

WHAT KIND OF DIET?

A full-scale elimination diet involves eating a very limited range of bland foods that rarely, if ever, trigger any kind of allergy or intolerance. This might include such things as chicken, peas and potatoes, with a few variants such as lamb, rice, broccoli, pears and rhubarb to relieve the monotony. Your diet will usually need to be boosted with vitamin and mineral supplements to ensure adequate nutrition. Individual food items are then added to the diet, one at a time, to test for any reaction. This is clearly a time-consuming and unattractive process for most people, but there is a less drastic alternative that will be sufficient for the majority of people. It consists of a low-allergen diet which is far less restrictive than an elimination diet. Life is much simpler in this case because it means you concentrate on excluding one type of food – such as milk and dairy products – which is why it is worth doing some advance detective work to try and identify any foods that seem to trigger your symptoms before beginning such a diet.

ABOVE: As part of your preparation, avoid drinks containing caffeine, such as coffee, tea and colas.

PLANNING YOUR DIET

To get yourself in peak condition before you begin, take a critical look at what you normally eat. Unless your diet is already very healthy, you'll need to cut out nutritionally poor foods and avoid items that may have an adverse effect on your system. For most people, this means avoiding 'junk' food which is usually high in fat and may contain a lot of additives and salt, keeping processed foods to a minimum and substituting them with fresh foods, especially fruit and vegetables, lightly cooked or raw whenever possible. Cut out sugar, caffeine and alcohol, and opt for foods that are low in saturated fats. Try to stick to this eating plan for about three or four weeks before moving on to the next phase. You will find the guidelines and recipes in Chapter 8, pages 100–123, useful if you're stuck for healthy eating ideas.

The next stage is to decide which group of foods you want to exclude and plan your menus for the next two or three weeks. It's worth doing this so that you can shop for the right ingredients, and you will be less tempted to cheat if you have planned your meals in advance. It is important that you don't cheat, because eating something from your range of forbidden foods during this phase will mask any changes in your symptoms and make it impossible to judge whether excluding your suspect foods is affecting your symptoms one way or the other.

Your task will inevitably be more difficult if you eat food prepared by other people, so you may prefer to avoid eating out during this phase.

THE EXCLUSION PHASE

You will need to acquire a pretty detailed knowledge of the various possible disguises in which your forbidden foods can present themselves. For example, if you're excluding all dairy foods, it is not sufficient to avoid milk, cheese, yogurt and the like; you will also need to study the labels on any prepared foods to look for ingredients derived from milk. These may be listed as casein, caseinate, whey, lactalbumin, lactose or buttermilk, for example. Many people who react to cows' milk are also likely to respond to goats' milk, and possibly to soya milk, so steer clear of those too. Similarly, if you're cutting out wheat, you need to watch out for ingredients such as cereal binders and fillers, edible starch and hydrolized vegetable protein. Try to have as varied a diet as possible, and plan your menus so you don't eat the same food too often.

During this phase, you should continue to keep your detailed diary of what you eat and any change in your symptoms. It's not unusual to find you actually feel worse than before during the first few days of your new regime as your body adjusts to doing without foods it is used to. Once you have started to feel better (if you do), you can begin the reintroduction phase. If you are going to experience any improvement, it is likely to become noticeable by the end of two weeks. This may not happen at all if you are excluding the wrong group of foods or if you are also sensitive to something you are continuing to eat. And there will obviously be no change either if food is not, in fact, playing any role in your symptoms.

THE REINTRODUCTION PHASE

Once the improvement has continued for a couple of days, start to eat the forbidden foods again. Only reintroduce one at a time, and eat it for two consecutive days to see whether it triggers any reaction. It is best to introduce the food in its simplest form to begin with – pure milk or a breakfast cereal made from wheat alone, for example – so that the picture is not confused by the presence of any other ingredients. When you are sure all is well, you can go through the same process with another food. Any symptoms provoked by a particular food are likely to appear within 24–48 hours; if this happens, wait until they have gone completely before continuing with your reintroduction programme.

Depending on the extent of the foods you are testing, you should be in a position to recognize which foods, if any, affect you within a few weeks. Little or no improvement might mean that you are sensitive to a wider range of foods than those you have been testing. The only way to establish this is to go on a more severe elimination diet, but this is best done under the guidance of a dietician.

ABOVE: Pulses, such as lentils and chickpeas, are a good source of low-fat protein.

healthy eating

It's a sad fact of modern life that we increasingly regard food as a necessary fuel to be consumed with the minimum inconvenience and fuss. Survey after survey shows that we are spending less time on food preparation and cooking, while the sales of ready-made meals and takeaways are soaring. Yet there is no shortage of recipe books or even television cooks to teach us the pleasures to be had from devoting just a little more time and effort to what we put inside us. You don't have to spend hours in the kitchen to prepare enjoyable – and healthy – meals; all it takes is a bit of rethinking and advance planning.

Nutritionists largely agree on the kind of diet that promotes good health and that may even help to stave off some of the more major illnesses such as heart disease and some kinds of cancer. However, because research in this field tends to encourage apparently contradictory stories in papers, magazines and the television news, many people have given up taking any notice at all on the grounds that everything they enjoy is bad for them according to one expert or another. This is far from being the case, and a healthy diet can be easy to organize and enjoyable, provided you follow a few simple guidelines.

FOODS TO ENJOY

In health terms, the ideal diet consists largely of a variety of fresh foods which will supply all our needs in terms of energy, vitamins and minerals. In particular, nutritionists emphasize the importance of a high intake of fruit and vegetables, either fresh or frozen, and you should aim to have five portions every day, not counting potatoes. Eating plenty of fruit and vegetables will help to ensure that you get sufficient vitamins, including vitamin C and beta-carotene (which is turned into vitamin A in the body) which are antioxidants: that is, they help to get rid of free radicals. These chemicals are generated in the body in response partly to cigarette smoke and other airborne pollutants and can play a part in triggering inflammation in the airways.

Red, orange and yellow fruits and vegetables contain high levels of beta-carotene. Vitamin C may also promote good lung health and help the airways to resist narrowing. Vitamin E, which is found in sunflower seeds, margarine and oil, as well as in soya beans and olive oil, is another anti-oxidant and so may also be beneficial to people with asthma. A very recent UK study found that eating five or more apples every week was associated with an improved lung function. The researchers suggest that

TOP: Red, orange and yellow fruits and vegetables contain substances that may help to reduce inflammation.

ABOVE: It is preferable to get vitamins and minerals from food rather than supplements, if possible.

this might be due to an antioxidant called querticin found in hard but not soft fruits. Apples are a particularly rich source, but it is also present in onions, tea and red wine. Dark green vegetables, together with peas and courgettes, are good sources of magnesium (as are fish and sunflower seeds). There is evidence to suggest that this mineral may help to relax the airways and that people with low levels may be more susceptible to asthma attacks.

Other important minerals include zinc, selenium, magnesium and manganese; your body's requirements should be met if you include fish and shellfish, nuts, pulses, milk, cheese and eggs in your diet on a regular basis (provided you are not allergic or intolerant to any of them).

Research suggests that getting your vitamins and minerals from food is more beneficial than taking supplements, possibly because other substances contained naturally in foods enhance their effectiveness.

FOODS TO AVOID

Unless you have your own reasons to choose to be a vegetarian or vegan, there is no need to stop eating meat altogether when trying to follow a healthy eating plan. Liver is an excellent source of vitamin A, for example, and eating other kinds of meat is one of the simplest ways to safeguard your intake of important minerals such as zinc, selenium and manganese. However, it is worth opting for leaner cuts of red meat or poultry, to ensure that you keep calories derived from fat down to the recommended maximum of 30 per cent of your daily energy intake. Wherever possible, you should substitute monounsaturated or polyunsaturated fats (those that are liquid at room temperature, apart from coconut and palm oil) for saturated fats, which are derived from animal sources. These help to reduce the risk of heart disease and are an important source of the fat-soluble vitamins (A, D, E and K) and of the essential fatty acids omega-3 and omega-6 which are vital to many body functions and can only be obtained through food sources.

The other main food group that you need to cut down on is the so-called extrinsic sugars. This means ordinary table sugar (sucrose), both white and brown, honey, glucose and syrups, but does not include the sugars naturally present in fruits and many root vegetables, for example. Extrinsic sugars contain no nutrients although, because they are rapidly absorbed, they can produce a quick burst of energy. The disadvantage is that your body responds to the sudden rise in blood glucose levels by turning up insulin production to cope, and the resultant slump in blood glucose can leave you feeling worse than before.

elimination recipes

An elimination diet stands a much bigger chance of successfully identifying the possible role of food in triggering your symptoms if you have some suspicions as to the possible culprits. **By avoiding a particular group or groups of food and keeping a careful record of the responses, you should be able to judge whether the process is helpful within two or three weeks**. While it is not particularly difficult to exclude one or two food groups completely for this length of time, excluding more may be difficult and could mean you risk missing out on vital nutrients. **It can be done however, provided you pay careful attention to the vitamin and mineral content of the meals you choose**, and ensure that you eat sufficient protein to meet your body's needs. If in doubt, explain to your doctor what you are planning to do and see if it is possible to get advice from a dietician.

You may find it helps to avoid any food you normally eat a lot of and, especially, any for which you have cravings. This can sometimes be an indication that you are allergic to or intolerant of that particular item. If you find your symptoms are no better by the end of two to three weeks, food may not be a factor or you may be sensitive to many different foods and would benefit from a more rigorous exclusion diet supervised by a dietician.

pumpkin soup

Serves 4 – Preparation time: 25 minutes – Cooking time: 1¼ hours

Per serving – Energy: 380 kcals/1599 kJ · Protein: 14 g · Carbohydrate: 55 g · Fat: 13 g · Fibre: 6 g

✔ alcohol free
✔ citrus free
dairy free
gluten free
wheat free

1	**tablespoon sunflower or olive oil**
1	**large onion, finely chopped**
3	**garlic cloves, crushed**
2	**celery sticks, chopped**
750 g	**(1½ lb) pumpkin flesh,**
	roughly chopped
750 ml	**(1¼ pints) vegetable or chicken stock**
	pinch of grated nutmeg
1	**bay leaf**
	a few parsley stalks
65 ml	**(2½ fl oz) single cream**
1–2	**tablespoons finely chopped parsley,**
	plus extra to garnish
	salt and pepper

To Garnish:
1	**small French stick**
50 g	**(2 oz) Gruyère or fontina cheese, grated**

1 Heat the oil in a saucepan and fry the onion and garlic until soft but not brown. Add the celery and pumpkin flesh and fry for 10–15 minutes. Stir in the stock and nutmeg. Tie the bay leaf and parsley stalks together with string, add to the saucepan and bring to the boil. Reduce the heat and simmer for about 30 minutes until the vegetables are soft.

2 Remove the herbs and purée the soup in a food processor or blender, or pass it through a fine sieve. Return the purée to the saucepan, bring to the boil and season with salt and pepper. Stir in the cream and parsley, reheat to just below boiling point, then reduce the heat. Keep it warm while preparing the garnish.

3 Cut 8 slices from the French bread, place on a baking sheet and toast under a preheated moderate grill until pale golden on both sides. Leave the grill on.

4 Pour the hot soup into 4 deep ovenproof bowls. Arrange 2 pieces of bread in each one. Sprinkle the bread with cheese. Set the bowls on the baking sheet and cook quickly under the grill until the cheese is golden brown.

tomatoes with fennel and dill

Serves 4 – Preparation time: 15 minutes – Cooking time: 15 minutes

Per serving – Energy: 40 kcals/172 kJ · Protein: 2 g · Carbohydrate: 6 g · Fat: 1 g · Fibre: 3 g

4	small fennel heads
1	teaspoon olive oil
500 g	(1 lb) tomatoes, skinned and sliced
3	tablespoons chopped dill
	salt and pepper

1 Cut the fennel into very thin slices. Brush the bottom of a nonstick pan with a little of the oil and stew the fennel gently, stirring frequently, until almost soft. Add salt and pepper to taste.

2 Add the tomatoes to the fennel and continue cooking gently for 5 minutes, stirring occasionally, without breaking up the tomatoes. When cooked, stir in the chopped dill and transfer to a dish to cool. Serve at room temperature.

alcohol free	✔
citrus free	✔
dairy free	✔
gluten free	✔
wheat free	✔

guacamole

Serves 4 – Preparation time: 20 minutes

Per serving – Energy: 196 kcals/810 kJ · Protein: 3 g · Carbohydrate: 4 g · Fat: 19 g · Fibre: 1 g

2	large ripe avocados
3	tablespoons lemon or lime juice
2	garlic cloves, crushed
40 g	(1½ oz) spring onions, chopped
1–2	tablespoons chopped mild green chillies
125 g	(4 oz) tomatoes, skinned, deseeded and chopped
	salt and pepper
	rind of 1 lime, cut into strips, to garnish
8	corn tortilla chips
	oil for frying
1	tablespoon paprika

1 Cut the avocados in half and remove the stones. Scoop out the flesh into a bowl, add the lemon or lime juice and mash coarsely.

2 Add the garlic, spring onions and chillies, and season to taste. Mix in the chopped tomatoes. Cover and chill in the refrigerator for at least 1 hour.

3 Meanwhile, make the tortilla chips. Cut each tortilla into 8 equal-sized pieces. Heat the oil to 180–190°C (350–375°F) or until a cube of bread browns in 30 seconds. Add the tortilla chips and deep-fry until crisp and golden. Drain on absorbent kitchen paper and sprinkle with a little paprika and salt.

4 Serve the guacamole as a dip with the corn tortilla chips, if your diet allows, or vegetable crudités.

alcohol free	✔
citrus free	
dairy free	✔
gluten free	✔
wheat free	✔

zucchini al forno

Serves 4 – Preparation time: 15 minutes, plus cooling – Cooking time: 55 minutes

Per serving – Energy: 79 kcals/332 kJ · Protein: 6 g · Carbohydrate: 7 g · Fat: 4 g · Fibre: 1 g

4	**large or 8 small courgettes**
1	**teaspoon oil**
1	**garlic clove, finely chopped**
500 g	**(I lb) canned tomatoes**
50 g	**(2 oz) canned anchovies, drained**
	salt and pepper

To Garnish:
1 teaspoon chopped thyme
1 teaspoon chopped rosemary

To Serve:
lemon wedges
mixed salad

1 Slice the courgettes in half lengthways and scoop out the seeds and pulp with a teaspoon. Sprinkle the inside of each courgette with salt and leave to drain upside down on absorbent kitchen paper.

2 Heat the oil in a saucepan and lightly fry the garlic, then add the tomatoes. Bring to the boil and cook vigorously until reduced by half. Remove from the heat and stir in one chopped anchovy fillet. Season with salt and pepper to taste.

3 Wipe the insides of the courgettes with absorbent kitchen paper to remove the salt and set them in a large baking dish. Fill each one with some tomato sauce and arrange an anchovy fillet on top. Grind over plenty of black pepper and bake in a preheated oven at 200°C (400°F), Gas Mark 6, for about 40 minutes. Allow to cool, then garnish with thyme and rosemary and serve with lemon wedges and mixed salad leaves.

greek stuffed vine leaves

Serves 4 – Preparation time: 15 minutes – Cooking time: 30 minutes

Per serving – Energy: 190 kcals/803 kJ · Protein: 13 g · Carbohydrate: 15 g · Fat: 7 g · Fibre: 5 g

2	**tablespoons olive oil**
150 g	**(5 oz) lean minced beef**
1	**large onion, finely chopped**
¼	**fennel bulb, grated**
2	**garlic cloves, crushed**
150 g	**(5 oz) cooked long-grain rice**
1	**tablespoon chopped dill**
1	**teaspoon dried oregano**
425 g	**(14 oz) can vine leaves,**
	rinsed and drained
150 ml	**(¼ pint) dry red wine**
150 ml	**(¼ pint) water**
4	**tablespoons lemon juice**
	salt and pepper
	lemon wedges, to serve

1 Heat half the oil in a large frying pan. Add the minced meat, onion, fennel and garlic and fry, stirring, for 8–10 minutes until cooked. Stir in the rice, dill and oregano and season with salt and pepper to taste.

2 Divide the mixture evenly between the vine leaves. Fold the long sides of the vine leaves over the mixture, then roll them up securely from the shorter edge to make neat parcels.

3 Mix the remaining oil, wine, water and lemon juice in a saucepan. Add the stuffed vine leaves, cover and cook over a gentle heat for about 20 minutes. Remove with a slotted spoon and serve with lemon wedges.

alcohol free	
citrus free	
dairy free	✔
gluten free	✔
wheat free	✔

stir-fried chinese cabbage

Serves 4 – Preparation time: 10 minutes – Cooking time: 8 minutes

Per serving – Energy: 85 kcals/353 kJ · Protein: 4 g · Carbohydrate: 6 g · Fat: 6 g · Fibre: 1 g

✔ alcohol free
  citrus free
✔ dairy free
✔ gluten free
✔ wheat free

8–10	Chinese cabbage leaves
2	tablespoons oil
125 g	(4 oz) canned bamboo shoots, rinsed, drained and sliced
1	onion, sliced
1	celery stick, sliced
1	tablespoon lemon juice
	salt and pepper
	lemon slices, to garnish

1 Cut the Chinese cabbage leaves diagonally into thin strips.

2 Heat the oil in a nonstick frying pan or wok. Add all the vegetables and fry gently for about 8 minutes, stirring frequently. Add the lemon juice and season with salt and pepper to taste. Garnish with lemon slices and serve.

balsamic braised leeks and peppers

Serves 4 – Preparation time: 5 minutes – Cooking time: 20 minutes

Per serving – Energy: 70 kcals/288 kJ · Protein: 2 g · Carbohydrate: 5 g · Fat: 5 g · Fibre: 3 g

2 **tablespoons olive oil**
2 **leeks, cut into 2 cm (1 inch) pieces**
1 **orange pepper, cored, deseeded and cut into 2 cm (1 inch) chunks**
1 **red pepper, cored, deseeded and cut into 2 cm (1 inch) chunks**
3 **tablespoons balsamic vinegar**
handful of flat leaf parsley, chopped
salt and pepper

1 Heat the oil in a saucepan, add the leeks and peppers and stir well, then cover the pan and cook gently for 10 minutes.

2 Add the balsamic vinegar and cook for a further 10 minutes without a lid. The vegetables should be brown from the vinegar and all their liquid should have evaporated.

3 Season well with salt and pepper and stir in the chopped parsley just before serving.

alcohol free	✔
citrus free	✔
dairy free	✔
gluten free	✔
wheat free	✔

potted pork

Serves 8 – Preparation time: 10 minutes, plus cooling – Cooking time: 4½ hours

Per serving – Energy: 245 kcals/1017 kJ · Protein: 13 g · Carbohydrate: 0 g · Fat: 22 g · Fibre: 0 g

100 g **(4 oz) pork back fat, cut into small pieces**
500 g **(1 lb) boneless pork (use equal quantities of lean and fatty pork)**
2 **tablespoons water**
1 **bouquet garni**
1 **teaspoon ground mixed spice**
2–3 **garlic cloves (optional)**
salt and pepper
gluten free toasted bread, to serve

1 Put the pork fat in a heavy pan over a gentle heat for about 30 minutes until melted.

2 Meanwhile, cut the boned pork into small cubes, mixing the lean and fatty meat together. Add the pork to the pan with the water, bouquet garni, mixed spice, garlic, if using, and salt and pepper to taste.

3 Cover the pan and cook very gently for 4 hours, stirring occasionally. At the end of the cooking time the pork should have become extremely soft.

4 Pour the meat and fat into small earthenware pots and leave to cool. The fat will rise to the surface of the pots and solidify, sealing the meat. Cover the pots and store in the refrigerator until needed. Serve with lightly toasted gluten free bread.

alcohol free	✔
citrus free	✔
dairy free	✔
gluten free	✔
wheat free	✔

penne primavera

Serves 4 – Preparation time: 20 minutes – Cooking time: 15 minutes

Per serving – Energy: 488 kcals/2072 kJ · Protein: 18 g · Carbohydrate: 97 g · Fat: 6 g · Fibre: 9 g

✔ alcohol free
✔ citrus free
✔ dairy free
  gluten free
  wheat free

125 g	**(4 oz) broccoli, broken into small pieces**
125 g	**(4 oz) French beans,**
	cut into 5 cm (2 inch) lengths
125 g	**(4 oz) mangetout**
2	**tablespoons chopped herbs**
500 g	**(1 lb) penne**
	Vinaigrette:
3	**teaspoons olive oil**
2	**tablespoons cider or wine vinegar**
2	**teaspoons French mustard**
	or 1 teaspoon English mustard
1	**teaspoon caster sugar**
	freshly grated nutmeg (optional)
1	**garlic clove, crushed (optional)**
	salt and pepper

1 Steam the vegetables for 2–4 minutes until slightly softened but still brightly coloured and crisp. Drain and put into a large bowl.

2 To make the vinaigrette, blend together all the ingredients and pour over the vegetables. Sprinkle the herbs on top.

3 Meanwhile, cook the pasta in a large saucepan of boiling salted water for 10–12 minutes, or according to the packet instructions, until tender. Drain and mix with the vegetables and vinaigrette. Serve hot or cold.

pasta syracuse

Serves 6 – Preparation time: 15 minutes – Cooking time: about 30 minutes
Per serving – Energy: 362 kcals/1533 kJ · Protein: 13 g · Carbohydrate: 71 g · Fat: 5 g · Fibre: 7 g

1	large onion, sliced
2	garlic cloves, crushed
500 g	(1 lb) courgettes chopped
1	green pepper, cored, deseeded and chopped
400 g	(13 oz) can tomatoes, drained and roughly chopped
125 g	(4 oz) black olives, pitted
3	anchovy fillets, finely chopped
1	tablespoon chopped parsley, plus extra to garnish
2	teaspoons chopped marjoram
500 g	(1 lb) low-fat pasta
	salt and pepper

1 Heat a large frying pan or wok and dry-fry the onion and garlic for 5 minutes, turning constantly, until soft. Add the courgettes and cook for 10 minutes. Add the green pepper, tomatoes, olives, anchovies, parsley, marjoram and salt and pepper to taste. Bring to the boil, stirring. Cover the pan and simmer while cooking the pasta.

2 Cook the pasta in a large saucepan of boiling salted water for 10–12 minutes, or according to the packet instructions, until tender. Drain well and place in a warmed serving dish. Add the sauce and toss lightly together. Garnish with parsley and serve immediately.

alcohol free	✔
citrus free	✔
dairy free	✔
gluten free	
wheat free	

pasta with uncooked tomato sauce and basil

Serves 4 – Preparation time: 10 minutes, plus standing – Cooking time: about 12 minutes
Per serving – Energy: 370 kcals/1577 kJ · Protein: 12 g · Carbohydrate: 74 g · Fat: 5 g · Fibre: 6 g

500 g	(1 lb) ripe plum tomatoes, skinned
4	teaspoons olive oil
1	garlic clove, crushed
1	bunch of basil, stalks removed
375 g	(12 oz) penne, conchiglie or farfalle
	salt

1 Put the tomatoes into a food processor or blender and purée briefly. Alternatively, pass through them through a fine sieve. Add the oil and crushed garlic.

2 Tear the basil leaves into small pieces and add to the sauce. Leave the sauce to stand for about 30 minutes, then add salt to taste and stir well.

3 Cook the pasta in a large saucepan of boiling salted water for 10–12 minutes, or according to the packet instructions, until tender. Drain and transfer to a warmed serving dish. Pour the sauce over the pasta and serve immediately.

alcohol free	✔
citrus free	✔
dairy free	✔
gluten free	
wheat free	

quick vegetable curry

Serves 4 – Preparation time: 20 minutes – Cooking time: 25–30 minutes

Per serving – Energy: 258 kcals/1081 kJ · Protein: 7 g · Carbohydrate: 39 g · Fat: 9 g · Fibre: 9 g

✔ alcohol free
✔ citrus free
✔ dairy free
✔ gluten free
✔ wheat free

2	tablespoons sunflower oil
250 g	(8 oz) onions, sliced
1	garlic clove, chopped
1	cooking apple, peeled, cored and chopped
2.5 cm	(1 inch) piece of fresh root ginger, peeled and grated
2	tablespoons wheat-free curry powder
450 ml	(¾ pint) vegetable stock
250 g	(8 oz) potatoes, peeled and diced
250 g	(8 oz) carrots, peeled and sliced
250 g	(8 oz) pumpkin, peeled, deseeded and cubed
250 g	(8 oz) cauliflower florets
250 g	(8 oz) runner beans, sliced
50 g	(2 oz) sultanas
1	tablespoon grated fresh coconut
	salt and pepper
	rice, to serve

1 Heat the oil in a large pan. Add the onions, garlic, apple and ginger and fry gently for 5 minutes, stirring occasionally. Stir in the curry powder and fry gently for a further 3 minutes, stirring constantly.

2 Add the stock and bring to the boil, stirring constantly, until the sauce thickens slightly. Add salt and pepper to taste, then lower the heat and simmer for 2 minutes.

3 Add the potatoes and carrots. Cover the pan and simmer for 10 minutes.

4 Add the pumpkin, cauliflower, beans and sultanas. Cover and simmer for 5–10 minutes or until the cauliflower is just tender but still crisp and not broken up.

5 Sprinkle with the coconut and serve hot with rice.

green herb risotto

Serves 4 – Preparation time: 5 minutes – Cooking time: 25–30 minutes

Per serving – Energy: 425 kcals/1791 kJ · Protein: 11 g · Carbohydrate: 69 g · Fat: 13 g · Fibre: 2 g

✔ alcohol free
✔ citrus free
  dairy free
✔ gluten free
✔ wheat free

1 litre	(1¾ pints) vegetable stock
25 g	(1 oz) butter
1	tablespoon olive oil
1	onion, finely chopped
1	garlic clove, chopped
300 g	(10 oz) arborio rice
	handful of parsley, chopped
	handful of basil, chopped
	handful of oregano, chopped
	handful of thyme, chopped
50 g	(2 oz) Parmesan cheese, grated
	salt and pepper
	sage sprigs, to garnish

1 Heat the stock in a saucepan until gently simmering.

2 Melt the butter with the oil in a separate saucepan, add the onion and garlic and fry gently for 3 minutes.

3 Add the rice, stir well to coat the grains with the butter and oil, then add a ladleful of hot stock, enough to cover the rice, and stir well. Simmer gently and stir the rice constantly, adding more stock as it is absorbed. Continue adding the stock and stirring until it has all been absorbed and the rice is cooked and coated in a creamy sauce.

4 Add the chopped herbs and Parmesan. Season with salt and pepper, and stir well. Serve immediately, garnished with sage sprigs.

courgette and bean provençal

Serves 4 – Preparation time: 15 minutes, plus soaking – Cooking time: 1 hour 20 minutes

Per serving – Energy: 287 kcals/1205 kJ · Protein: 13 g · Carbohydrate: 38 g · Fat: 10 g · Fibre: 2 g

175 g	**(6 oz) cannellini beans, soaked overnight**
3	**tablespoons olive oil**
2	**onions, sliced**
2	**garlic cloves, chopped**
500 g	**(1 lb) courgettes, diced**
400 g	**(13 oz) can chopped tomatoes**
2	**tablespoons tomato purée**
2	**teaspoons chopped oregano**
1	**bouquet garni**
50 g	**(2 oz) black olives, halved and pitted**
	salt and pepper
	oregano sprigs, to garnish

1 Drain the beans, put them in a large saucepan, cover with fresh water and bring to the boil. Cover and simmer for 45–60 minutes until almost tender, adding salt towards the end of the cooking time. Drain, reserving 150 ml (¼ pint) of the cooking liquid.

2 Heat the oil in the saucepan and fry the onions until soft but not browned. Add the garlic and courgettes and fry gently, stirring occasionally, for a further 15 minutes.

3 Add the tomatoes, tomato purée, oregano, bouquet garni, salt and pepper, the drained beans and reserved liquid. Cover and simmer gently for 20 minutes, adding the olives 5 minutes before the end of the cooking time. Serve immediately, garnished with oregano.

alcohol free	✔
citrus free	✔
dairy free	✔
gluten free	✔
wheat free	✔

turkey risotto

Serves 4 – Preparation time: 10 minutes – Cooking time: about 30 minutes

Per serving – Energy: 463 kcals/1963 kJ · Protein: 34 g · Carbohydrate: 69 g · Fat: 8 g · Fibre: 3 g

✔	alcohol free
✔	citrus free
✔	dairy free
✔	gluten free
✔	wheat free

1.3 l (2¼ pints) turkey or vegetable stock
1 tablespoon olive oil
1 onion, finely chopped
350 g (12 oz) cooked turkey
125 g (4 oz) button mushrooms, sliced
1 small green pepper,
   cored, deseeded and sliced
300 g (10 oz) arborio rice
   salt and pepper
   crisp salad, to serve

1 Heat the stock in a saucepan until gently simmering.

2 Heat the oil in a large pan and gently fry the onion until tender. Add the turkey, mushrooms, green pepper, rice and salt and pepper to taste. Fry gently for a further 1–2 minutes, stirring to coat the added ingredients.

3 Add a ladleful of hot stock, enough to cover the rice, and stir well. Simmer gently and stir the rice constantly, adding more stock as it is absorbed. Continue adding the stock and stirring until it has all been absorbed and the rice is cooked and coated in a creamy sauce. Serve immediately with a crisp salad.

griddled and roasted guinea fowl

Serves 4 – Preparation time: 10 minutes – Cooking time: about 40 minutes

Per serving – Energy: 365 kcals/1536 kJ · Protein: 58 g · Carbohydrate: 1 g · Fat: 14 g · Fibre: 0 g

✔	alcohol free
	citrus free
✔	dairy free
✔	gluten free
✔	wheat free

1.75 kg (3½ lb) guinea fowl,
   jointed into 8 pieces
2 tablespoons Dijon mustard
   grated rind and juice of 2 lemons
1 teaspoon vegetable oil
   sea salt flakes and pepper
   lemon rind strips, to garnish
   griddled sweet potato slices, to serve
   (optional)

1 Heat a griddle pan until hot, put on the guinea fowl joints and cook for about 6 minutes on each side. The skin should be quite charred to give a good flavour.

2 Mix the mustard, lemon rind and juice together and season with salt and pepper.

3 Remove the guinea fowl from the pan and place it in a lightly oiled roasting tin. Using a pastry brush, brush the joints with the mustard mixture, then cook on the top shelf of a preheated oven at 200°C (400°F), Gas Mark 6, for 20 minutes. To test if cooked, insert a sharp knife into the thickest part of each joint – the juices should run clear.

4 Serve the guinea fowl garnished with strips of lemon rind, with griddled slices of sweet potato, if liked.

rabbit casserole

Serves 4 – Preparation time: 15 minutes – Cooking time: about 1 hour 40 minutes

Per serving – Energy: 245 kcals/1022 kJ · Protein: 24 g · Carbohydrate: 16 g · Fat: 10 g · Fibre: 3 g

2	tablespoons millet flour
2	tablespoons sunflower oil
4	rabbit joints, about 150 g (5 oz) each
2	onions, roughly chopped
3	carrots, peeled and roughly chopped
1	small turnip or swede, peeled and roughly chopped
½	teaspoon dried mixed herbs
300 ml	(½ pint) water
	salt and pepper

1 Season the flour with salt and pepper. Heat the oil in a frying pan. Coat the rabbit joints in the seasoned flour and fry gently until lightly browned all over. Remove and drain on absorbent kitchen paper, then transfer to an ovenproof casserole.

2 Add the onions, carrots, turnip or swede and mixed herbs. Pour over the water and cover. Cook in a preheated oven at 190°C (375°F), Gas Mark 5, for 1½ hours.

alcohol free	✔
citrus free	✔
dairy free	✔
gluten free	✔
wheat free	✔

duck with honey and fruit

Serves 4 – Preparation time: 25 minutes – Cooking time: 2½ hours

Per serving – Energy: 230 kcals/963 kJ · Protein: 9 g · Carbohydrate: 27 g · Fat: 10 g · Fibre: 4 g

1	duckling, about 2½ kg (5 lb)
1	small onion, peeled
2	tablespoons clear honey
1	tablespoon boiling water
	salt and pepper
	Salad:
4	crisp lettuce leaves
1	small radicchio
4	curly endive leaves
2	large peaches, sliced
1	small ripe pineapple, peeled and sliced
	handful of watercress
3	tablespoons olive oil
3	tablespoons white wine vinegar

1 Remove the giblets from the duckling. Rinse the duckling under cold running water, drain and pat dry with absorbent kitchen paper. Prick the skin all over with a fork. Sprinkle the body cavity with pepper and insert the onion. Place the bird, breast side up, on a rack in a roasting tin and sprinkle with salt. Roast in the centre of a preheated oven at 180°C (350°F), Gas Mark 4, for 2½ hours or until cooked through.

2 After 1 hour of cooking, pour off the fat from the tin. Blend the honey with the water and spoon over the duck. Continue cooking, basting the duck two or three times with juices from the tin.

3 After 2½ hours of cooking, check that the juices run clear when the thigh is pierced with a fine skewer, then remove the duck from the oven and cool.

4 Divide the salad ingredients between 4 plates. Mix the oil and vinegar together and season with salt and pepper, then sprinkle the dressing over the salad. Serve with the cold duck.

alcohol free	✔
citrus free	✔
dairy free	✔
gluten free	✔
wheat free	✔

pork steaks with okra

Serves 4 – Preparation time: 10 minutes – Cooking time: about 25 minutes

Per serving – Energy: 302 kcals/1261 kJ · Protein: 38 g · Carbohydrate: 3 g · Fat: 16 g · Fibre: 2 g

✔ alcohol free
✔ citrus free
✔ dairy free
✔ gluten free
✔ wheat free

4	**pork steaks, about 175 g (6 oz) each**
1	**tablespoon sunflower oil**
2	**tomatoes, skinned, quartered and deseeded**
2	**teaspoons tomato purée**
150 ml	**(¼ pint) water**
125 g	**(4 oz) okra, stalk ends trimmed**
	salt and pepper
	watercress sprigs, to garnish

1 Wipe the pork steaks dry with absorbent kitchen paper. Heat the oil in a large frying pan, add the steaks and fry over a moderate heat until well browned on both sides. Remove the steaks from the pan with a slotted spoon and place in a warmed serving dish. Keep hot.

2 Add the remaining ingredients to the pan and cook for 8 minutes, stirring occasionally, until the okra is just tender. Pour over the pork and serve garnished with watercress sprigs.

mediterranean lamb casserole

Serves 4 – Preparation time: 10 minutes – Cooking time: 1 hour 10 minutes

Per serving – Energy: 275 kcals/1153 kJ · Protein: 28 g · Carbohydrate: 4 g · Fat: 17 g · Fibre: 2 g

✔ alcohol free
✔ citrus free
✔ dairy free
✔ gluten free
✔ wheat free

2	**tablespoons sunflower oil**
500 g	**(1 lb) lean boneless leg of lamb, cut into 2.5 cm (1 inch) cubes**
400 g	**(13 oz) can tomatoes**
150 ml	**(¼ pint) water**
1	**rosemary sprig**
1	**thyme sprig**
1	**bay leaf**
125 g	**(4 oz) mushrooms, sliced**
1	**green pepper, cored, deseeded and sliced**
	salt and pepper
	chopped parsley, to garnish

1 Heat the oil in an ovenproof casserole or heavy-based pan. Add the lamb and cook, stirring frequently, for 5 minutes or until evenly browned. Stir in the tomatoes with their juice and the water. Add the herbs and seasoning to taste. Stir well, then cover and simmer for 45 minutes.

2 Add the sliced mushrooms and green pepper to the casserole. Check the seasoning, cover and simmer the dish gently for a further 20 minutes.

3 Discard the herbs. Sprinkle with chopped parsley and serve.

spinach-stuffed lamb

Serves 4 – Preparation time: 20 minutes – Cooking time: 45–55 minutes

Per serving – Energy: 256 kcals/1074 kJ · Protein: 28 g · Carbohydrate: 4 g · Fat: 11 g · Fibre: 0 g

250 g	(8 oz) spinach, cooked, drained and chopped
15 g	(½ oz) mint, finely chopped
4	garlic cloves, finely chopped
1	teaspoon vinegar
	pinch of sugar
1	half leg of lamb (knuckle end), boned
175 ml	(6 fl oz) red wine
	salt and pepper
	chopped parsley, to garnish

To Serve:
salad leaves
shredded carrot

1 Mix the spinach with the mint, garlic, vinegar and sugar and season with salt and pepper.

2 Trim every scrap of fat from the lamb. Lay it flat with the boned side up, and spread over the spinach mixture. Fold over the meat and secure with string as if tying a parcel. Place the meat in a roasting tin and pour over the wine, adding a little water if the tin is much larger than the meat. Cook in a preheated oven at 180°C (350°F), Gas Mark 4, for 45–55 minutes.

3 Transfer to a hot carving plate and cut into thick slices. Pour off the excess fat from the roasting tin and pour the remaining juices around the lamb, sprinkle with parsley. Serve with salad leaves and shredded carrot.

alcohol free	
citrus free	✔
dairy free	✔
gluten free	✔
wheat free	✔

venison steaks with redcurrant and cranberry sauce

Serves 4 – Preparation time: 10 minutes, plus marinating – Cooking time: about 25 minutes
Per serving – Energy: 273 kcals/1162 kJ · Protein: 39 g · Carbohydrate: 23 g · Fat: 3 g · Fibre: 1 g

	alcohol free
	citrus free
✔	dairy free
✔	gluten free
✔	wheat free

1   teaspoon juniper berries, crushed
4   fillet or loin venison steaks,
      about 175 g (6 oz) each
      sea salt flakes and pepper

Sauce:
125 g   (4 oz) redcurrant jelly
125 g   (4 oz) cranberries
      grated rind and juice of 1 orange
2   tablespoons red wine

1   Mix the juniper berries with salt and pepper and spread over both sides of the venison steaks. Set aside to absorb the flavours for at least 1 hour or preferably overnight.

2   To make the sauce, place the ingredients, reserving half of the orange rind for garnishing, in a small saucepan and simmer gently for about 10 minutes, stirring constantly.

3   Heat a griddle pan or nonstick frying pan until hot. Put on the venison steaks and cook for 3 minutes on each side for rare, 5 minutes for well done. Serve immediately with the redcurrant and cranberry sauce, garnish with the reserved orange rind.

poached salmon steaks with hot basil sauce

Serves 6 – Preparation time: 15 minutes – Cooking time: 25 minutes

Per serving – Energy: 266 kcals/1105 kJ · Protein: 24 g · Carbohydrate: 2 g · Fat: 17 g · Fibre: 1 g

1	**large bunch of basil**
4	**celery sticks, chopped**
1	**carrot, chopped**
1	**small courgette, chopped**
1	**small onion, chopped**
6	**salmon steaks, about 125 g (4 oz) each**
75 ml	**(3 fl oz) dry white wine**
125 ml	**(4 fl oz) water**
1	**teaspoon lemon juice**
15 g	**(½ oz) unsalted butter**
	salt and pepper
	lemon slices, to serve

1 Strip the leaves from half the basil and set aside. Spread all the chopped vegetables over the bottom of a large flameproof casserole dish with a lid, press the salmon steaks into the vegetables and cover them with the remaining basil, reserving a few leaves for garnishing. Pour over the wine and water and season with salt and pepper. Bring to the boil, cover and simmer for about 10 minutes. Transfer the salmon to a warmed serving dish.

2 Bring the poaching liquid and vegetables back to the boil and simmer for 5 minutes. Strain into a food processor or blender and add the cooked and uncooked basil. Blend to a purée and return to a saucepan. Bring the purée to the boil and reduce by half, until thickened. Remove the saucepan from the heat, add the lemon juice and stir in the butter. Pour the sauce over the salmon steaks, garnish with the reserved basil leaves and serve with lemon slices.

alcohol free	
citrus free	
dairy free	
gluten free	✔
wheat free	✔

lychee and apricot compôte

Serves 6 – Preparation time: 20 minutes, plus soaking and chilling – Cooking time: 20 minutes

Per serving – Energy: 163 kcals/692 kJ · Protein: 3 g · Carbohydrate: 31 g · Fat: 4 g · Fibre: 8 g

✔ alcohol free
  citrus free
✔ dairy free
✔ gluten free
✔ wheat free

425 g	(14 oz) canned lychees
175 g	(6 oz) dried apricots
2	large oranges
2	tablespoons pine nuts, toasted

1 Drain the lychees and make up the liquid to 300 ml (½ pint) with water. Put the apricots into a saucepan, pour over the liquid, cover and bring to the boil. Turn off the heat and leave to soak for 1 hour. Bring to the boil again, cover, simmer gently for 10 minutes and leave to cool. Turn into a glass bowl with the lychees.

2 Pare off thin slices of orange rind with a potato peeler and cut them into needle-fine shreds. Blanch in boiling water for 1 minute, then drain and dry on absorbent kitchen paper.

3 Peel the oranges with a serrated knife and cut into segments, removing all the membrane. Add to the bowl and mix together gently.

4 Sprinkle the fruit with the pine nuts and orange rind, and serve chilled.

tropical fruit salad

Serves 4–6 – Preparation time: 15 minutes, plus chilling – Cooking time: 7 minutes

Per serving – Energy: 163 kcals/694 kJ · Protein: 2 g · Carbohydrate: 39 g · Fat: 1 g · Fibre: 5 g

2 **kiwi fruits, peeled and sliced**
1 **starfruit, sliced**
2 **mangoes, peeled and cubed**
1 **small papaya, peeled and cubed**
6 **lychees, peeled and stoned**
1 **banana, sliced**
   lime rind strips, to garnish

   Dressing:
25 g **(1 oz) sugar**
100 ml **(3½ fl oz) water**
2 **tablespoons lime juice**
   pulp and seeds of 2 passion fruits

1 First make the dressing. Put the sugar and water in a saucepan and heat until the sugar has dissolved. Add the lime juice and simmer for 5 minutes. Remove from the heat and set aside to cool. When the dressing is cool, stir in the passion fruit pulp and seeds.

2 Gently mix all the prepared fruit in a large bowl. Pour the dressing over the fruit and chill for 15 minutes. Serve garnished with lime rind strips.

alcohol free ✔
citrus free
dairy free ✔
gluten free ✔
wheat free ✔

honeyed breakfast cereal

Serves 12 – Preparation time: 10 minutes, plus cooling – Cooking time: 20 minutes

Per serving – Energy: 330 kcals/1390 kJ · Protein: 6 g · Carbohydrate: 57 g · Fat: 10 g · Fibre: 3 g

4 **tablespoons sunflower or safflower oil**
250 g **(8 oz) clear honey**
250 g **(8 oz) millet, rye or barley flakes**
250 g **(8 oz) rolled oats**
50 g **(2 oz) sesame seeds**
50 g **(2 oz) dried peaches, pears or figs, chopped**
125 g **(4 oz) sultanas or seedless raisins**
50 g **(2 oz) pumpkin seeds**
   milk or milk substitute, yogurt, fresh fruit or fruit juice, to serve

1 Warm the oil in a large roasting tin. Stir in the honey, flakes and oats. Add the sesame seeds and cook in a preheated oven at 180°C (350°F), Gas Mark 4, for 20 minutes. Stir the mixture occasionally so that it browns evenly.

2 Remove from the oven and allow to cool, then mix in the dried fruit and pumpkin seeds. Store in an airtight container.

3 Serve with milk or milk substitute, yogurt, fresh fruit or fruit juice.

alcohol free ✔
citrus free
dairy free
gluten free ✔
wheat free ✔

individual fruit tarts

Makes 12 – Preparation time: 20 minutes, plus cooling – Cooking time: 20 minutes

Per tart – Energy: 118 kcals/494 kJ · Protein: 1 g · Carbohydrate: 16 g · Fat: 6 g · Fibre: 1 g

✔ alcohol free
✔ citrus free
✔ dairy free
  gluten free
  wheat free

250 g	**(8 oz) sweet shortcrust pastry**
300 g	**(10 oz) prepared fresh fruit (eg pineapple, grapes, cherries, melon or peaches)**
125 g	**(4 oz) apricot or cherry jam (additive-free, sugar-reduced variety)**
1	**tablespoon water**

1 Roll out the pastry to a thickness of 5 mm (¼ inch). Cut out the tart cases with a pastry cutter, arrange them in lightly greased patty tins and prick the bases. Fill with foil and baking beans. Bake blind in a preheated oven at 200°C (400°F), Gas Mark 6, for about 15 minutes or until crisp and golden. Remove the foil and baking beans and allow the tarts to cool.

2 When cold, fill the tarts with fruit, arranged attractively.

3 Make a glaze by heating the jam and water together in a saucepan over a gentle heat until the jam softens. Pass through a sieve and glaze the tarts with the mixture.

pineapple upside-down cake

Serves 8 – Preparation time: 15 minutes – Cooking time: 30 minutes

⅛ cake – Energy: 186 kcals/788 kJ · Protein: 3 g · Carbohydrate: 39 g · Fat: 3 g · Fibre: 2 g

	oil, for greasing
100 g	(3½ oz) potato flour
25 g	(1 oz) soya flour
75 g	(3 oz) brown rice flour
2	apples, grated
50 g	(2 oz) raw cane sugar
1	tablespoon wheat-free baking powder
200 ml	(7 fl oz) pineapple juice
1	tablespoon sunflower oil

Topping:

250 g	(8 oz) can pineapple slices in natural juice (juice reserved for the cake)
40 g	(1½ oz) raw cane sugar
4–5	fresh cherries, stoned

1 Lightly grease a straight-sided, 23 cm (9 inch) round ovenproof dish with oil. For the topping, arrange the pineapple slices on the base and sprinkle the sugar over the top. Cut the cherries in half and arrange them between the pineapple slices.

2 Put the remaining ingredients in a food processor or blender and blend until creamy. Spread over the pineapple and cherries.

3 Bake in a preheated oven at 200°C (400°F), Gas Mark 6, for 30 minutes. Leave to cool for 5 minutes, then turn out on to a serving plate. Serve hot or cold.

alcohol free	✔
citrus free	✔
dairy free	✔
gluten free	✔
wheat free	✔

pears in cassis

Serves 4 – Preparation time: 10 minutes – Cooking time: 25 minutes

Per serving – Energy: 113 kcals/482 kJ · Protein: 1 g · Carbohydrate: 29 g · Fat: 0 g · Fibre: 3 g

300 ml	(½ pint) apple juice
125 g	(4 oz) blackcurrants, stalks removed
	honey, to taste
1	cinnamon stick
4	pears
1	teaspoon arrowroot

1 Pour the apple juice into a pan. Add the blackcurrants, honey and cinnamon. Heat gently until the honey has dissolved, then bring to the boil. Boil for 1 minute.

2 Peel the pears, leaving the stalks attached. Put the pears in the pan, submerging them as much as possible in the blackcurrant mixture. Cover and cook gently for about 20 minutes until the pears are tender, turning them occasionally.

3 Lift the pears from the pan and transfer to a serving bowl. Discard the cinnamon stick.

4 Blend the arrowroot with a little cold water, then pour into the blackcurrant mixture. Bring to the boil, then lower the heat and simmer for 1 minute until the sauce thickens, stirring constantly. Pour over the pears. Serve hot or cold.

alcohol free	✔
citrus free	✔
dairy free	✔
gluten free	✔
wheat free	✔

Following a healthy eating plan means considering what you include on your daily menus as well as what you cut out. It is important to exclude everything which might counteract the beneficial effects of this way of eating even though you may not be allergic to, or intolerant of, them specifically. **As far as possible, you should focus on fresh food with the minimum of additives and try to steer clear of prepared dishes or 'instant' items** such as ready-made sauces, toppings and spreads, unless they are made from a few pure and wholesome ingredients. **Caffeine, alcohol and chocolate in particular can all have adverse effects on the body**, while sugar in any form can cause your blood glucose levels to rise and fall rapidly without supplying any nutritional benefits other than calories.

Try to think in terms of building each meal around some form of complex carbohydrate – such as pasta or rice – with vegetables and/or fruit, and a minimum of protein. It is better to have a relatively small quantity of low-fat protein such as lean meat, poultry or pulses than a large serving of a high-fat protein – such as shoulder of pork – with vegetables as an accompaniment.

minted green pea soup with paprika

Serves 6 – Preparation time: 20 minutes – Cooking time: 30–45 minutes

Per serving – Energy: 154 kcals/647 kJ · Protein: 9 g · Carbohydrate: 16 g · Fat: 7 g · Fibre: 9 g

✔ alcohol free
citrus free
dairy free
✔ gluten free
✔ wheat free

1	**tablespoon olive or sunflower oil**
1	**onion, chopped**
2	**celery sticks, chopped**
1–2	**teaspoons hot paprika,**
	plus extra to garnish
900 ml	**(1½ pints) vegetable or chicken stock**
750 g	**(1½ lb) fresh or frozen peas**
3	**mint sprigs, plus extra to garnish**
1	**tablespoon lime juice**
150 ml	**(¼ pint) half-fat crème fraîche**
	salt and pepper
	croûtons, to garnish (optional)

1 Heat the oil in a large saucepan and fry the onion and celery until soft but not brown. Stir in the paprika and fry for a few minutes. Add the stock with the peas, mint and lime juice. Bring to the boil, then reduce the heat and simmer for 15–20 minutes until the peas are tender. If using frozen peas, cook for only 5–8 minutes. Do not overcook the peas or the soup will lose its bright green colour.

2 When the peas are soft, blend the soup in a food processor or blender until smooth. Alternatively, pass the soup through a fine sieve. Return the purée to the saucepan, bring to the boil and season with salt and pepper to taste. Remove from the heat and stir in two-thirds of the crème fraîche, then add a little extra stock or water if necessary, to give the desired consistency. Warm through gently.

3 Serve the soup in shallow soup bowls with the croûtons, if using, and a spoonful of the remaining crème fraîche in the centre of each bowl. Sprinkle a little paprika on top and garnish with a sprig of mint.

vermicelli and bean soup

Serves 6 – Preparation time: 10 minutes, plus soaking – Cooking time: about 2 hours

Per serving – Energy: 250 kcals/1059 kJ · Protein: 13 g · Carbohydrate: 41 g · Fat: 5 g · Fibre: 11 g

250 g	(8 oz) red kidney beans, soaked overnight and drained
1.8 l	(3 pints) water
4	tablespoons tomato purée
2	tablespoons olive oil
1	onion, chopped
1	garlic clove, crushed
3	celery sticks, chopped
3	carrots, sliced
2	tomatoes, skinned and chopped
2	tablespoons chopped parsley
1	teaspoon dried oregano
125 g	(4 oz) vermicelli, broken into short lengths
	salt and pepper

1 Bring the beans, water and tomato purée to the boil in a large pan. Cover and simmer for 1½ hours.

2 Heat a wok and dry-fry the onion and garlic for 3–6 minutes. Transfer to a baking dish and soften in a pre-heated oven, 180°C (350°F), Gas Mark 4, for 6 minutes.

3 Add the garlic and onion mixture to the beans with the vegetables and herbs. Season, cover and simmer for 20 minutes.

4 Add the pasta to the pan and cook for 5 minutes until *al dente*. Serve immediately.

alcohol free	✔
citrus free	✔
dairy free	✔
gluten free	
wheat free	

potato, celery and apple salad

Serves 6 – Preparation time: 20 minutes, plus cooling – Cooking time: 20–25 minutes

Per serving – Energy: 195 kcals/820 kJ · Protein: 9 g · Carbohydrate: 21 g · Fat: 9 g · Fibre: 3 g

✔ alcohol free
citrus free
dairy free
✔ gluten free
✔ wheat free

500 g	**(1 lb) new potatoes**
2	**crisp dessert apples, cored and sliced**
1	**tablespoon lemon juice**
1	**celery head, thinly sliced**
125 g	**(4 oz) half-fat Cheddar cheese, diced**
1	**red onion, thinly sliced**
2	**tablespoons wine vinegar**
2	**tablespoons apple juice**
1	**teaspoon mild French mustard**
	pinch of sugar
3	**tablespoons sunflower oil**
	salt and pepper
	dill or chervil sprigs, to garnish

1 Cook the potatoes in lightly salted boiling water for 20–25 minutes until just tender. Drain and allow to cool, then cut them carefully into 5 mm (¼ inch) slices.

2 Sprinkle the apples with a little of the lemon juice. Mix together the potatoes, apples, celery, cheese and onion. In a small bowl, beat together the remaining lemon juice, vinegar, apple juice, mustard, sugar and oil. Season with salt and pepper to taste. Pour the dressing over the potato mixture and mix thoroughly. Serve garnished with dill or chervil sprigs.

melon and prawn cocktail

Serves 4 – Preparation time: 15 minutes – Cooking time: 10–12 minutes

Per serving – Energy: 263 kcals/1110 kJ · Protein: 17 g · Carbohydrate: 37 g · Fat: 6 g · Fibre: 3 g

125 g (4 oz) pasta spirals
2 tomatoes, skinned and cut into 8 pieces
½ honeydew melon, cubed
175 g (6 oz) cooked peeled prawns
½ cucumber, cubed
½ teaspoon cayenne pepper, to garnish

Dressing:
3 tablespoons low-fat mayonnaise
1 tablespoon tomato ketchup
3 tablespoons low-fat natural yogurt
salt and pepper

1 Cook the pasta in a large saucepan of boiling salted water for 10–12 minutes, or according to packet instructions, until tender. Rinse under cold running water and drain well.

2 Mix the pasta, tomatoes, melon, prawns and cucumber together in a bowl. To make the dressing, mix together the mayonnaise, ketchup and yogurt, and season with salt and pepper. Pour the dressing over the pasta mixture and toss well. To serve, spoon into glasses and sprinkle each with a little cayenne pepper.

alcohol free	✔
citrus free	✔
dairy free	
gluten free	
wheat free	

winter salad

Serves 6 – Preparation time: 15 minutes, plus cooling – Cooking time: about 12 minutes

Per serving – Energy: 215 kcals/905 kJ · Protein: 13 g · Carbohydrate: 28 g · Fat: 7 g · Fibre: 3 g

175 g (6 oz) pasta bows
175 g (6 oz) cooked skinless chicken, diced
2 celery sticks, diced
2 red dessert apples, cored and diced
1 green pepper, cored, deseeded and diced
4 tablespoons low-fat mayonnaise
salt and pepper
½ lettuce, to serve

1 Cook the pasta bows in a large saucepan of boiling salted water for 10–12 minutes, or according to the packet instructions, until tender. Rinse under cold running water and drain well.

2 Mix the chicken with the celery, apples, green pepper and pasta bows, and season to taste with salt and pepper. Fold in the mayonnaise and turn into a salad bowl on a bed of lettuce.

alcohol free	✔
citrus free	✔
dairy free	
gluten free	
wheat free	

emerald green salad

Serves 4–6 – Preparation time: 20 minutes

Per serving – Energy: 322 kcals/1328 kJ · Protein: 3 g · Carbohydrate: 8 g · Fat: 31 g · Fibre: 1 g

1 cos lettuce
2 ripe avocados, peeled and stoned
2 tablespoons lemon juice
3 kiwi fruits, peeled and cut into wedges
2 tablespoons chopped fresh mixed herbs (mint, parsley, basil, chives)
2 spring onions, sliced

French Dressing:
2 tablespoons red or white wine vinegar
1–2 garlic cloves, crushed
2 teaspoons Dijon mustard
¼ teaspoon caster sugar
6 tablespoons olive oil
salt and pepper

1 First make the dressing. Put all the ingredients in a screw-top jar, close the lid tightly and shake well until thoroughly combined. Use as required.

2 Tear the lettuce into bite-sized pieces and place in a large salad bowl. Chop the avocado flesh and place in a bowl with the lemon juice. Toss well, then add to the salad bowl.

3 Add the kiwi fruits to the salad, along with the chopped herbs and the spring onions.

4 Finally, give the French dressing a last shake, pour over the salad and toss lightly.

rustic greek salad

Serves 8 – Preparation time: 15 minutes

Per serving – Energy: 155 kcals/644 kJ · Protein: 6 g · Carbohydrate: 4 g · Fat: 13 g · Fibre: 2 g

750 g (1½ lb) tomatoes (large, cherry or miniature plum)
250 g (8 oz) feta cheese, drained and cut into 1 cm (½ inch) cubes
1 small red onion, cut into 16 wedges
16 black Kalamata olives
25 flat leaf parsley leaves
2 tablespoons lemon juice
4 tablespoons light extra virgin olive oil
salt and pepper

1 If using large tomatoes, cut each into 6 wedges. If using smaller tomatoes, cut them in half lengthways. Put into a large bowl with the feta. Scatter over the onion wedges, olives and parsley leaves.

2 Pour over the lemon juice and toss very gently to coat, using 2 wooden spoons or your fingers so as not to break the tomato flesh or the cheese. Pour over the oil, toss again and season with salt and pepper to taste. Serve the salad immediately.

hot thai beef salad

Serves 4 – Preparation time: 15 minutes – Cooking time: 5 minutes
Per serving – Energy: 307 kcals/1289 kJ · Protein: 31 g · Carbohydrate: 24 g · Fat: 10 g · Fibre: 7 g

1	**crisp lettuce, shredded**
75 g	**(3 oz) bean sprouts**
2	**ripe papayas, peeled and thinly sliced**
½	**large cucumber, cut into matchsticks**
4	**spring onions, cut into matchsticks**
2	**tablespoons vegetable oil**
500 g	**(1 lb) rump or fillet steak,**
	cut into thin strips across the grain
3	**garlic cloves, finely chopped**
2	**green chillies, thinly sliced**
8	**tablespoons lemon juice**
1	**tablespoon Thai fish sauce**
2	**teaspoons sugar**

1 Place a pile of lettuce and bean sprouts on 4 individual plates and arrange the papaya, cucumber and spring onions to one side. Cover loosely and set aside.

2 Heat the oil in a heavy-based frying pan or wok over a moderate heat until hot. Add the beef, garlic and chillies, increase the heat to high and stir-fry for 3–4 minutes or until browned on all sides. Pour in the lemon juice and fish sauce, add the sugar and stir-fry until sizzling.

3 Remove the wok from the heat. Remove the beef from the dressing with a slotted spoon and divide between the 4 piles of lettuce and bean sprouts arranging the papaya to one side and the cucumber and spring onions on top. Pour over the dressing and serve immediately.

alcohol free	✔
citrus free	
dairy free	✔
gluten free	✔
wheat free	✔

paglia e fieno with tomato and rosemary

Serves 4 – Preparation time: 15 minutes – Cooking time: about 50 minutes

Per serving – Energy: 306 kcals/1228 kJ · Protein: 11 g · Carbohydrate: 53 g · Fat: 5 g · Fibre: 2 g

alcohol free
✔ citrus free
✔ dairy free
gluten free
wheat free

625 g **(1¼ lb) canned tomatoes**
1 **tablespoon olive oil**
1 **small carrot, finely chopped**
1 **small onion, finely chopped**
1 **celery stick, finely chopped**
4 **tablespoons red wine**
2 **whole dried red chillies**
300 g **(10 oz) fresh paglia e fieno pasta**
2 **teaspoons chopped rosemary**
salt and pepper
rosemary sprigs, to garnish

1 Purée the tomatoes and their juice in a food processor or blender.

2 Heat the oil in a heavy saucepan. Add the carrot, onion and celery and cook gently, stirring frequently, for 15 minutes or until soft. Add the wine, increase the heat and stir until the wine has been absorbed by the vegetables. Add the puréed tomatoes and the whole chillies, then season to taste and bring to the boil. Reduce the heat, cover and simmer for 15–20 minutes until the sauce is quite thick.

3 Meanwhile, cook the pasta in a large saucepan of boiling salted water for 3–4 minutes, or according to the packet instructions, until tender. Drain the pasta and turn it into a warmed bowl. Remove the sauce from the heat and stir in the chopped rosemary. Adjust the seasoning, if necessary. Pour the sauce over the pasta and serve garnished with rosemary sprigs.

fettuccine with walnut sauce

Serves 4 – Preparation time: 10 minutes – Cooking time: 15 minutes

Per serving – Energy: 379 kcals/1595 kJ · Protein: 15 g · Carbohydrate: 50 g · Fat: 15 g · Fibre: 4 g

250 g	(8 oz) fettuccine
1	tablespoon olive oil
50 g	(2 oz) walnuts
1	bunch of chives
175 g	(6 oz) fat-free fromage frais
25 g	(1 oz) Parmesan cheese, grated
	salt
	chive flowers, to garnish

1 Cook the pasta in a large saucepan of boiling salted water for 10–12 minutes, or according to the packet instructions, until tender. Drain and toss in the oil, then transfer to a warmed serving dish and keep warm.

2 Finely chop the walnuts and chives and mix together.

3 Put the fromage frais into a heavy-based saucepan and heat very gently, taking care not to let it boil. Stir in the Parmesan, the walnuts and chives and heat through. Pour over the pasta and garnish with chive flowers.

alcohol free	✔
citrus free	✔
dairy free	
gluten free	
wheat free	

vegetable couscous

Serves 4 – Preparation time: 15 minutes, plus soaking – Cooking time: 50 minutes

Per serving – Energy: 545 kcals/2286 kJ · Protein: 19 g · Carbohydrate: 90 g · Fat: 14 g · Fibre: 5 g

2	tablespoons olive oil
2	onions, sliced
1	teaspoon ground cinnamon
1	teaspoon turmeric
1	teaspoon ground ginger
½	teaspoon chilli powder
2	garlic cloves, crushed
2	carrots, diced
125 g	(4 oz) broad beans
475 g	(15 oz) canned chickpeas, drained
2	tablespoons tomato purée
600 ml	(1 pint) vegetable stock
375 g	(12 oz) couscous
50 g	(2 oz) raisins
2	courgettes, sliced
125 g	(4 oz) green beans, cut into 2.5 cm (1 inch) lengths
2	whole canned tomatoes, cut into 8 pieces
2	tablespoons chopped parsley
2	tablespoons blanched almonds, toasted
	salt and pepper

1 Heat the oil in a large saucepan, over which you can later fit a steamer. Add the onions and fry until softened. Add the spices and garlic and cook for 1 minute.

2 Add the carrots, broad beans, chickpeas and tomato purée with the stock, bring to the boil, season with salt and pepper to taste and cook for 20 minutes.

3 Meanwhile, put the couscous into a bowl, cover with water and leave for 15 minutes. Drain, mix in the raisins and put into a steamer or colander lined with muslin.

4 Add the courgettes, green beans, tomatoes and parsley to the vegetables and stir well. Fit the steamer or colander over the saucepan, making sure the bottom does not touch the stew. Steam, covered, for 20 minutes, until the vegetables are tender and the couscous is heated through.

5 Turn the couscous on to a serving dish, separating the grains with a fork. Spoon the vegetables on top and sprinkle with the almonds. Serve the sauce separately.

alcohol free	✔
citrus free	✔
dairy free	✔
gluten free	
wheat free	

bean tagine

Serves 8 – Preparation time: 30 minutes, plus soaking – Cooking time: 2¾ hours

Per serving – Energy: 311 kcals/1310 kJ · Protein: 17 g · Carbohydrate: 42 g · Fat: 10 g · Fibre: 18 g

✔ alcohol free
✔ citrus free
✔ dairy free
✔ gluten free
✔ wheat free

500 g	(1 lb) red or white kidney beans, soaked overnight
2	celery sticks, halved
2	bay leaves
4	parsley sprigs
4	tablespoons olive oil
500 g	(1 lb) onions, chopped
5	garlic cloves, crushed
2	red chillies, deseeded and chopped
4	red peppers, cored, deseeded and chopped
1	tablespoon paprika
	large handful of mixed mint, parsley and coriander, chopped
	salt and pepper
	mint leaves, to garnish

Sauce:

1 kg	(2 lb) canned chopped tomatoes
2	tablespoons olive oil
4	parsley sprigs
1	tablespoon sugar

1 Drain the beans and boil in fresh, unsalted water for 10 minutes, then drain. Tie the celery, bay leaves and parsley together with kitchen string. Cover the beans with fresh unsalted water, add the celery and herbs and simmer for about 1 hour until the beans are just tender. Drain, reserving the cooking liquid, and discard the celery and herbs.

2 Meanwhile, make the sauce. Empty the tomatoes and their juice into a saucepan, add the oil, parsley and sugar and bring to the boil, then simmer, uncovered, for about 20 minutes until thick.

3 Heat the oil in a heavy flameproof casserole. Add the onions, garlic, chillies, red peppers and paprika and cook gently for 5 minutes. Stir in the beans, the sauce and enough of the reserved cooking liquid to just cover the beans. Season with salt and pepper, cover and cook in a preheated oven at 150°C (300°F), Gas Mark 2, for 1½ hours, stirring occasionally.

4 Just before serving, stir in the mint, parsley and coriander. Serve immediately, garnished with mint leaves.

spinach and chickpea flan

Serves 8 – Preparation time: 25 minutes, plus chilling – Cooking time: about 1 hour
Per serving – Energy: 246 kcals/1029 kJ · Protein: 7 g · Carbohydrate: 24 g · Fat: 14 g · Fibre: 1 g

300 g	(10 oz) shortcrust pastry
175 g	(6 oz) spinach leaves
1	tablespoon extra virgin olive oil
1	small onion, thinly sliced
2	garlic cloves, crushed
1	teaspoon ground turmeric
200 g	(7 oz) canned chickpeas, drained
2	eggs, lightly beaten
200 ml	(7 fl oz) semi-skimmed milk
	pinch of grated nutmeg
	salt and pepper

1 Roll out the pastry on a lightly floured surface and use to line a deep, 20 cm (8 inch) flan tin. Prick the base and chill for 20 minutes. Line with foil and fill with baking beans. Bake blind in a preheated oven at 200°C (400°F), Gas Mark 6, for 10 minutes. Remove the foil and beans and bake the pastry for 10–12 minutes more until crisp.

2 Meanwhile, wash the spinach and place in a large saucepan. Heat gently for 3–4 minutes until the spinach wilts. Drain, squeeze out the liquid and chop finely.

3 Heat the oil in a saucepan, add the onion, garlic and turmeric and fry for 5 minutes. Stir in the chickpeas and spinach. Spread the mixture over the pastry case.

4 Beat together the eggs, milk, nutmeg and salt and pepper and pour into the pastry case. Bake for 35–40 minutes until firm and golden. Serve hot or cold.

alcohol free	✔
citrus free	✔
dairy free	
gluten free	
wheat free	

cabbage, beetroot and apple sauté

Serves 4 – Preparation time: 20 minutes – Cooking time: about 55 minutes
Per serving – Energy: 296 kcals/1234 kJ · Protein: 5 g · Carbohydrate: 23 g · Fat: 18 g · Fibre: 6 g

40 g	(1½ oz) butter
½	red cabbage, thinly shredded
1	tablespoon chopped thyme
2	teaspoons caraway seeds
1	teaspoon ground mixed spice
1	tablespoon sugar
150 ml	(¼ pint) red wine
2	tablespoons port
2	tablespoons red wine vinegar
2	dessert apples, cored and thickly sliced
250 g	(8 oz) cooked beetroot, cubed
50 g	(2 oz) pecan nuts, toasted
	salt and pepper

1 Melt two-thirds of the butter in a large frying pan and fry the cabbage, thyme, caraway seeds, mixed spice and sugar for 10 minutes. Add the wine, port and vinegar and bring to the boil. Cover the pan and cook over a low heat for 20 minutes.

2 Meanwhile, melt the remaining butter in a clean frying pan and fry the apples for 4–5 minutes until lightly golden. Add to the cabbage with the pan juices and the beetroot. Cover and cook for a further 15–20 minutes until the cabbage is tender. Season with salt and pepper. Stir in the pecan nuts and serve immediately.

alcohol free	
citrus free	✔
dairy free	
gluten free	✔
wheat free	✔

mediterranean fish stew

Serves 6 – Preparation time: 15 minutes – Cooking time: 40 minutes

Per serving – Energy: 287 kcals/1203 kJ · Protein: 37 g · Carbohydrate: 9 g · Fat: 8 g · Fibre: 3 g

alcohol free

✔ citrus free

✔ dairy free

✔ gluten free

✔ wheat free

3	**tablespoons sunflower oil**
2	**onions, sliced**
2	**carrots, sliced**
3	**celery sticks, sliced**
125 g	**(4 oz) mushrooms, sliced**
2	**garlic cloves, crushed**
4	**tomatoes, skinned and chopped**
300 ml	**(½ pint) dry white wine**
600 ml	**(1 pint) fish or vegetable stock**
1	**bay leaf**
750 g	**(1½ lb) cod or haddock fillet, skinned and boned**
200 g	**(7 oz) jar mussels in brine, drained**
175 g	**(6 oz) cooked peeled prawns**
	salt and pepper
	chopped parsley, to garnish

1 Heat the oil in a large saucepan and add the onions, carrots, celery, mushrooms and garlic. Cook until softened, but not brown. Add the tomatoes, wine, stock and bay leaf. Season with salt and pepper to taste and simmer for 15 minutes.

2 Cut the fish into 5 cm (2 inch) cubes. Add to the saucepan and simmer for 15 minutes.

3 Add the mussels and prawns to the pan and simmer for a further 2–3 minutes.

4 To serve, turn the stew into a warmed serving dish and garnish with the chopped parsley.

spaghetti with mediterranean fish sauce

Serves 6 – Preparation time: 10 minutes – Cooking time: 25–30 minutes

Per serving – Energy: 375 kcals/1592 kJ · Protein: 27 g · Carbohydrate: 66 g · Fat: 2 g · Fibre: 6 g

1	small onion, finely chopped
2	garlic cloves, finely chopped
1	small red pepper, cored, deseeded and diced
1	small green pepper, cored, deseeded and diced
400 g	(13 oz) can chopped tomatoes
4	tablespoons finely chopped flat leaf parsley
500 g	(1 lb) cod, cut into cubes
500 g	(1 lb) spaghetti
	salt and pepper

1 Heat a wok and dry-fry the onion, garlic and peppers for 3–6 minutes, turning constantly, until soft.

2 Stir in the tomatoes, parsley and fish, and season to taste. Simmer, uncovered, until the fish is just tender.

3 Meanwhile, cook the pasta in a large saucepan of boiling salted water for 10–12 minutes, or according to the packet instructions, until tender. Drain and toss well with half of the sauce. Transfer to a warm serving dish. Spoon the remaining sauce over the top of the pasta and serve immediately.

alcohol free	✔
citrus free	✔
dairy free	✔
gluten free	
wheat free	

stir-fried seafood with vegetables

Serves 4 – Preparation time: 20 minutes – Cooking time: 5 minutes

Per serving – Energy: 200 kcals/840 kJ · Protein: 17 g · Carbohydrate: 12 g · Fat: 9 g · Fibre: 1 g

4–6	scallops
150 g	(5 oz) raw tiger prawns, peeled and deveined
1	egg white
1	tablespoon cornflour
	vegetable oil, for deep-frying
3	celery sticks, sliced
1	red pepper, cored, deseeded and sliced
1–2	carrots, peeled and sliced
2	slices fresh root ginger, peeled and shredded
2–3	spring onions, chopped
2	tablespoons sherry
1	tablespoon light soy sauce
2	teaspoons chilli bean paste (optional)
1	teaspoon salt
1	teaspoon sesame oil

1 Cut each scallop into 3 or 4 pieces. Cut the prawns into 2 or 3 pieces, if large. Put the seafood in a bowl with the egg white and half of the cornflour, and mix well.

2 Heat the oil in a wok and deep-fry the scallops and prawns for 1 minute, stirring all the time to keep the pieces separate. Remove with a perforated spoon and drain on absorbent kitchen paper.

3 Pour off all but 2 tablespoons of oil from the wok. Increase the heat to high and add the vegetables, ginger and spring onions. Stir-fry for about 1 minute. Add the scallops and prawns and stir in the sherry, soy sauce, chilli bean paste, if using, and salt.

4 Mix the remaining cornflour to a smooth paste with a little water, then add to the wok. Stir well until thickened. Sprinkle over the sesame oil and serve immediately.

alcohol free	
citrus free	✔
dairy free	✔
gluten free	✔
wheat free	✔

spinach and chicken cannelloni

Serves 6 – Preparation time: 20 minutes – Cooking time: 1¼ hours

Per serving – Energy: 270 kcals/1142 kJ · Protein: 22 g · Carbohydrate: 37 g · Fat: 4 g · Fibre: 1 g

✔ alcohol free
✔ citrus free
dairy free
gluten free
wheat free

12	**dried cannelloni tubes**
25 g	**(1 oz) half-fat Cheddar cheese, grated**
	Filling:
250 g	**(8 oz) spinach leaves**
2	**onions, finely chopped**
150 g	**(5 oz) cooked chicken breast, minced**
125 g	**(4 oz) low-fat cottage cheese**
1	**teaspoon ground cinnamon**
	salt and pepper
	Tomato Sauce:
1	**tablespoon chopped oregano**
300 ml	**(½ pint) passata (sieved tomatoes)**
½	**teaspoon caster sugar**
	Cheese Sauce:
15 g	**(½ oz) cornflour**
300 ml	**(½ pint) skimmed milk**
50 g	**(2 oz) low-fat Cheddar cheese, grated**

1 To prepare the filling, remove any tough stalks from the spinach and put it into a large saucepan with just the water that clings to the leaves after washing. Cook over a low heat for 5 minutes or until the leaves have wilted. Strain, squeeze out all the excess liquid and chop the spinach finely.

2 Heat a large frying pan or wok and dry-fry the onion for 3–6 minutes, stirring constantly, until soft. Add half of the onion to the spinach with the chicken, cottage cheese and cinnamon, and season to taste. Stir well and spoon into the cannelloni tubes, then arrange them in a single layer in a rectangular 1.2 litre (2 pint) ovenproof dish.

3 To make the tomato sauce, transfer the remaining onion to a saucepan and stir in the oregano, passata and sugar and simmer for 15 minutes.

4 To make the cheese sauce, mix the cornflour with a little milk, heat the remaining milk in a saucepan, then mix in the cornflour mixture. Simmer until thickened. Add the cheese and stir until melted.

5 Pour the tomato sauce over the filled cannelloni, followed by the cheese sauce. Sprinkle the grated cheese over the top. Bake in a preheated oven at 190°C (375°F), Gas Mark 5, for 45 minutes. Serve immediately.

garlic chicken with lemon sauce

Serves 4 – Preparation time: 15 minutes, plus marinating – Cooking time: 20–30 minutes
Per serving – Energy: 294 kcals/1233 kJ · Protein: 38 g · Carbohydrate: 7 g · Fat: 13 g · Fibre: <1 g

4	**boneless, skinless chicken breasts**
2	**tablespoons lemon juice**
1	**tablespoon sunflower oil**
	mangetout, to serve (optional)

Stuffing:

125 g	**(4 oz) curd cheese or quark**
2	**garlic cloves, finely chopped**
1	**tablespoon chopped thyme**
1	**tablespoon chopped rosemary**

Sauce:

25 g	**(1 oz) sunflower margarine**
25 g	**(1 oz) plain flour**
300 ml	**(½ pint) hot chicken stock**
2	**tablespoons lemon juice**
	salt and pepper

To Garnish:
lemon slices
rosemary sprigs

1 Place the chicken breasts between sheets of grease-proof paper and flatten with a rolling pin. Place in a large, shallow dish in a single layer. Mix the lemon juice and oil together and pour over the chicken breasts. Leave to marinate for 15 minutes, turning once or twice.

2 To make the stuffing, mix all the ingredients together in a bowl and season with pepper. Lift the chicken breasts out of the marinade with a slotted spoon. Reserve the marinade. Spread the stuffing over the chicken breasts, roll them up and secure with wooden cocktail sticks. Brush the marinade over the chicken breasts and cook under a preheated grill for 10–15 minutes on each side, brushing with more marinade as they cook.

3 Meanwhile, make the sauce. Melt the margarine in a small saucepan, stir in the flour and cook for 1 minute. Remove the saucepan from the heat and gradually add the stock, stirring well. Return to the heat and bring to the boil, stirring continuously. Allow to boil for 1–2 minutes. Add the lemon juice and heat through. Season with salt and pepper.

4 Thinly slice the chicken breasts when cooked and arrange on warmed serving plates. Serve with mangetout, if liked. Pour over the sauce and garnish with lemon slices and rosemary sprigs.

alcohol free	✔
citrus free	
dairy free	
gluten free	
wheat free	

liver and bacon with roasted tomato chutney

Serves 4 – Preparation time: 10 minutes – Cooking time: about 55 minutes

Per serving – Energy: 558 kcals/2334 kJ · Protein: 37 g · Carbohydrate: 33 g · Fat: 32 g · Fibre: 4 g

✔ alcohol free
✔ citrus free
✔ dairy free
✔ gluten free
✔ wheat free

3	tablespoons olive oil
750 g	(1½) lb tomatoes, halved and green cores removed
1	red onion, sliced
1	garlic clove, chopped
50 g	(2 oz) raisins
50 g	(2 oz) brown sugar
3	tablespoons white wine vinegar
1	teaspoon chopped rosemary
1	teaspoon black mustard seeds
8	smoked streaky bacon rashers, rinded
4	calves' liver slices, about 125 g (4 oz) each
	sea salt flakes and pepper
	rosemary sprigs, to garnish

1 Spoon 2 tablespoons of the olive oil into a roasting tin and heat in a preheated oven at 220°C (425°F), Gas Mark 7. Add the tomatoes, turning them in the oil to coat well, and place the tin at the top of the oven. Roast for 40 minutes, or until the tomatoes begin to darken around the edges.

2 Heat the remaining oil in a frying pan and add the onion and garlic. Gently fry for 5 minutes, then add the raisins, brown sugar, vinegar, rosemary, mustard seeds and seasoning. Mix well and simmer for 2 minutes. Mix in the roasted tomatoes, then remove from the heat.

3 Heat a griddle pan until hot, put on the bacon and cook for about 2 minutes on each side until crispy. Keep warm. Place the calves' liver on the griddle and cook for 2 minutes on each side for pink or 4 minutes for well done. Serve at once with the bacon and roasted tomato chutney, garnished with rosemary sprigs.

griddled gammon with apricot salsa

Serves 4 – Preparation time: 20 minutes – Cooking time: 25–35 minutes

Per serving – Energy: 349 kcals/1469 kJ · Protein: 52 g · Carbohydrate: 8 g · Fat: 12 g · Fibre: 1 g

4	**gammon steaks, about 175 g (6 oz) each**
250 g	**(8 oz) fresh apricots, stoned and chopped, or ready-to-eat dried apricots**
	grated rind and juice of 1 lime
2	**teaspoons grated fresh root ginger**
2	**teaspoons clear honey**
1	**tablespoon olive oil**
2	**tablespoons chopped sage**
4	**spring onions, finely chopped**
	sea salt flakes and pepper

1 Heat a griddle pan until hot. Put on the gammon steaks in batches and cook for 4 minutes on each side. Keep warm until they are all cooked.

2 Mix together the apricots, lime rind and juice, ginger, honey, oil and sage in a small bowl. Crush the mixture with the back of a fork. Add the spring onions and season, mixing well. Serve the steaks immediately with the apricot salsa.

alcohol free	✔
citrus free	
dairy free	✔
gluten free	✔
wheat free	✔

penne with chicken livers

Serves 4 – Preparation time: 10 minutes – Cooking time: 10–15 minutes

Per serving – Energy: 433 kcals/1826 kJ · Protein: 23 g · Carbohydrate: 60 g · Fat: 13 g · Fibre: 5 g

✔ alcohol free
✔ citrus free
 dairy free
 gluten free
 wheat free

1	yellow pepper, cored and deseeded
300 g	(10 oz) penne
1	tablespoon olive oil
25 g	(1 oz) butter
1	red onion, sliced
250 g	(8 oz) chicken livers, trimmed
1	rosemary sprig, chopped
	salt and pepper
25 g	(1 oz) Parmesan cheese, grated, to serve

1 Roast the pepper in a hot oven or under a preheated hot grill, skin-side up, until the skin is blackened. Allow to cool, then peel off the skin. Cut the flesh into strips.

2 Cook the pasta in a large saucepan of boiling salted water for 10–12 minutes, or according to the packet instructions, until tender. Drain well.

3 Meanwhile, heat the oil and butter in a large frying pan, add the onion and chicken livers and cook over a high heat until browned all over but still pink in the middle. Add the rosemary and pepper strips, and season well.

4 Mix the chicken liver mixture with the cooked pasta and toss well. Serve immediately with the Parmesan.

mixed chow mein

Serves 4 – Preparation time: 15 minutes – Cooking time: 10 minutes

Per serving – Energy: 690 kcals/2912 kJ · Protein: 28 g · Carbohydrate: 94 g · Fat: 25 g · Fibre: 10 g

✔ alcohol free
✔ citrus free
✔ dairy free
 gluten free
 wheat free

500 g	(1 lb) dried egg noodles
4	tablespoons vegetable oil
1	onion, thinly sliced
125 g	(4 oz) cooked meat (pork, chicken or ham), shredded
125 g	(4 oz) mangetout, trimmed
125 g	(4 oz) bean sprouts
2–3	spring onions, thinly shredded
2	tablespoons light soy sauce
1	tablespoon sesame oil or chilli sauce
	salt

1 Cook the noodles in a large saucepan of boiling salted water until tender but still firm. Drain in a colander and rinse under cold running water until cool. Set aside.

2 Heat about 3 tablespoons of the oil in a hot wok or frying pan. Add the onion, shredded meat, mangetout and bean sprouts, and stir-fry for 1 minute. Add 1 teaspoon of salt and stir a few more times. Remove from the wok with a perforated spoon and keep warm.

3 Heat the remaining oil in the wok. Add the spring onions and noodles with half the stir-fried mixture. Add the soy sauce and stir-fry for 1–2 minutes.

4 Transfer to a warmed serving dish and top with the remaining stir-fried mixture. Sprinkle with sesame oil or chilli sauce and serve immediately.

balti kheema

Serves 4 – Preparation time: 15 minutes – Cooking time: 35 minutes

Per serving – Energy: 422 kcals/1765 kJ · Protein: 42 g · Carbohydrate: 14 g · Fat: 23 g · Fibre: 4 g

2	**tablespoons vegetable oil**
500 g	**(1 lb) green peppers, cored, deseeded and sliced**
500 g	**(1 lb) onions, sliced**
2	**teaspoons salt**
2	**teaspoons pepper**
½	**teaspoon ground cumin**
2	**teaspoons garam masala pinch of ground cinnamon**
1½	**teaspoons chilli powder**
750 g	**(1½ lb) minced lamb red onion rings, to garnish poppadums, to serve**

1 Heat the oil in a Balti pan or heavy-based frying pan, add the peppers and stir-fry for about 1 minute. Remove the peppers with a slotted spoon and keep warm.

2 Add the onions to the oil and fry until they are golden brown. Add the salt, pepper, cumin, garam masala, cinnamon and chilli powder and stir-fry for 2 minutes.

3 Add the minced lamb and cook gently for about 20 minutes, stirring frequently to make sure that it does not stick to the bottom of the pan.

4 Return the peppers to the pan and heat through over a low heat for a further 10 minutes. Garnish with onion rings and serve with poppadums.

alcohol free	✔
citrus free	✔
dairy free	✔
gluten free	
wheat free	

spicy beef koftas in pizzaiola sauce

Serves 4 – Preparation time: 20 minutes – Cooking time: 1 hour

Per serving – Energy: 385 kcals/1616 kJ · Protein: 30 g · Carbohydrate: 31 g · Fat: 16 g · Fibre: 5 g

- ✔ alcohol free
- ✔ citrus free
- ✔ dairy free
- gluten free
- wheat free

1	tablespoon sunflower or olive oil
1	large onion, finely chopped
2	garlic cloves, crushed
1	red chilli, deseeded and finely chopped
2	red peppers, cored, deseeded and chopped
400 g	(13 oz) can plum tomatoes
300 ml	(½ pint) vegetable stock
2	tablespoons double-concentrate tomato purée
2	tablespoons finely chopped oregano pinch of sugar
1	tablespoon chopped flat leaf parsley
75 g	(3 oz) black Kalamata olives, pitted flat leaf parsley sprigs, to garnish boiled rice, to serve (optional)

Koftas:

1	medium egg
50 g	(2 oz) coarse breadcrumbs
500 g	(1 lb) lean minced beef
75 g	(3 oz) onion, grated
2	tablespoons plain flour
1	tablespoon sunflower or olive oil salt and pepper

1 First make the koftas. Beat the egg in a large bowl, stir in the breadcrumbs and add the beef and onion. Season with salt and pepper. Work the ingredients together until well combined. You will find that your hands are best for this. Divide the mixture into 8 portions, shape each one into a ball and roll in a little flour. Heat the oil in a large frying pan and fry the koftas until evenly browned, turning frequently. This will take about 10 minutes.

2 Meanwhile, prepare the sauce. Heat the oil in a saucepan and fry the onion and garlic until soft but not brown. Add the remaining ingredients, except half of the olives. Bring to the boil and cook over a high heat for 10 minutes.

3 Using a slotted spoon, lower the koftas into the sauce. Cover and cook gently for about 30 minutes until the meat is cooked through and the sauce is rich and pulpy. Remove about 50 ml (2 fl oz) of the sauce and a few olives and process to a thick purée in a food processor or blender. Stir back into the sauce. Season with salt and pepper to taste. Serve with rice, if liked, and garnish with the parsley sprigs and remaining olives.

beef tacos

Serves 4 – Preparation time: 20–25 minutes – Cooking time: about 30 minutes
Per serving – Energy: 333 kcals/1400 kJ · Protein: 27 g · Carbohydrate: 7 g · Fat: 6 g · Fibre: 1 g

500 g	**(1 lb) minced beef**
75 g	**(3 oz) onion, finely chopped**
65 g	**(2½ oz) green pepper, cored,**
	deseeded and finely chopped
1	**garlic clove, crushed**
1	**teaspoon dried oregano**
½	**teaspoon hot paprika**
¼	**teaspoon ground cumin**
¼	**teaspoon dried red hot pepper flakes**
125 ml	**(4 fl oz) tomato purée**
12	**corn taco shells**
	salt and pepper
	paprika, to garnish

To Serve:
shredded red cabbage
soured cream

1 Put the minced beef in a frying pan and fry it gently in its own fat until it is cooked and browned, breaking it up as it cooks. Pour off and discard any excess fat. Add the onion, green pepper and garlic and cook, stirring occasionally, until softened. Stir in the oregano, spices and salt and pepper to taste, then add the tomato purée and mix well. Cover and cook gently for 10 minutes, stirring occasionally.

2 Meanwhile, heat the taco shells in a preheated oven at 180°C (350°F), Gas Mark 4. Serve the beef filling in the hot corn taco shells, accompanied by shredded red cabbage and soured cream, and garnished with paprika.

alcohol free	✔
citrus free	✔
dairy free	
gluten free	✔
wheat free	✔

summer pudding

Serves 8 – Preparation time: 30 minutes, plus soaking and chilling – Cooking time: 15 minutes

Per serving – Energy: 116 kcals/494 kJ · Protein: 4 g · Carbohydrate: 25 g · Fat: 1 g · Fibre: 8 g

✔ alcohol free
✔ citrus free
✔ dairy free
gluten free
wheat free

500 g	(1 lb) mixed blackberries and blackcurrants
3	tablespoons clear honey
125 g	(4 oz) raspberries
125 g	(4 oz) strawberries
8	slices wholewheat bread, crusts removed
	low-fat yogurt, to serve (optional)

To Decorate:
redcurrants
mint sprigs

1 Place the blackberries, blackcurrants and honey in a heavy-based saucepan and cook gently for 10–15 minutes until tender, stirring occasionally. Add the raspberries and strawberries and leave to cool. Strain the fruit, reserving the juice.

2 Cut 3 circles of bread to fit the base, middle and top of a 900 ml (1½ pint) pudding basin. Shape the remaining bread to fit around the sides of the basin. Soak all the bread in the reserved fruit juice.

3 Line the bottom of the basin with the smallest circle of bread, then arrange the shaped bread around the sides. Pour in half of the fruit and place the medium-sized circle of bread on top. Cover with the remaining fruit, then top with the largest bread circle. Fold over any bread protruding from the basin.

4 Cover with a saucer small enough to fit inside the basin and put a 500 g (1 lb) weight on top. Leave in the refrigerator overnight. Turn on to a serving plate and pour over any remaining fruit juice. Decorate with redcurrants and mint sprigs, and serve with yogurt, if liked.

blackberry stuffed apples

Serves 4 – Preparation time: 10 minutes – Cooking time: 45 minutes

Per serving – Energy: 159 kcals/673 kJ · Protein: 1 g · Carbohydrate: 40 g · Fat: 0 g · Fibre: 7 g

4	**large cooking apples**
250 g	**(8 oz) blackberries**
4	**tablespoons raw cane sugar**
1	**tablespoon chopped mint**
4	**tablespoons water**

1 Remove the cores from the apples, making a large hole for the stuffing. Make a shallow cut through the skin around the centre of each apple to prevent the skins from bursting.

2 To make the stuffing, mix the blackberries with the sugar and mint. Place the apples in a baking dish and divide the stuffing equally between them, pressing it well down into the centres. Spoon any remaining stuffing around the apples, then spoon over the water.

3 Bake in a preheated oven at 180°C (350°F), Gas Mark 4, for 45 minutes or until the apples are tender. Serve hot.

alcohol free	✔
citrus free	✔
dairy free	✔
gluten free	✔
wheat free	✔

hot fruit salad

Serves 6 – Preparation time: 10 minutes, plus soaking – Cooking time: 10–15 minutes

Per serving – Energy: 229 kcals/970 kJ · Protein: 4 g · Carbohydrate: 46 g · Fat: 4 g · Fibre: 13 g

175 g	**(6 oz) dried apricots**
150 g	**(5 oz) dried prunes**
150 g	**(5 oz) dried figs**
600 ml	**(1 pint) apple juice**
2	**tablespoons Calvados or brandy (optional)**
25 g	**(1 oz) walnuts, coarsely chopped, to decorate**
	low-fat natural yogurt, to serve (optional)

1 Place the dried fruits in a bowl with the apple juice and leave to soak overnight.

2 Transfer to a saucepan and simmer for 10–15 minutes. Turn into a bowl and pour over the Calvados or brandy, if using. Sprinkle with walnuts and serve immediately with yogurt, if liked.

alcohol free	✔
citrus free	✔
dairy free	✔
gluten free	✔
wheat free	✔

applenut spice squares

Makes 9 squares – Preparation time: 15 minutes – Cooking time: 45–50 minutes

Per square – Energy: 227 kcals/955 kJ · Protein: 3 g · Carbohydrate: 35 g · Fat: 9 g · Fibre: 2 g

✔ alcohol free
✔ citrus free
dairy free
gluten free
wheat free

125 g	**(4 oz) flour**
1	**teaspoon bicarbonate of soda**
½	**teaspoon ground cinnamon**
	pinch of ground cloves
50 g	**(2 oz) sunflower margarine**
125 g	**(4 oz) golden granulated sugar**
1	**egg, beaten**
50 g	**(2 oz) walnuts, coarsely chopped**
75 g	**(3 oz) sultanas**
150 ml	**(¼ pint) apple purée (made from 500 g (1 lb) cooking apples)**
	icing sugar, to dust (optional)

1 Sieve the flour, bicarbonate of soda, cinnamon and cloves into a mixing bowl and mix together. Work in the margarine lightly with your fingers. Mix in the sugar and beaten egg. Add the walnuts, sultanas and apple purée, and blend well. Pour the mixture into a greased and lined 18 cm (7 inch) square tin.

2 Bake in the centre of a preheated oven at 180°C (350°F), Gas Mark 4, for 45–50 minutes or until firm to the touch. Cut into squares. Serve cold, dusted with icing sugar, if liked.

peach granita

Serves 4 – Preparation time: 15 minutes, plus freezing – Cooking time: 6 minutes

Per serving – Energy: 76 kcals/324 kJ · Protein: 3 g · Carbohydrate: 11 g · Fat: <1 g · Fibre: 3 g

375 g	**(12 oz) ripe peaches, peeled and chopped**
150 ml	**(¼ pint) dry white wine**
150 ml	**(¼ pint) orange juice**
2	**egg whites**
	redcurrants, to decorate

1 Put the peach flesh into a saucepan with the white wine and orange juice. Simmer gently for 5 minutes, then blend the peaches and liquid in a blender or food processor until smooth. Leave to cool.

2 Put the peach mixture into a shallow plastic container. Freeze until the granita is slushy around the edges, then tip into a bowl and break up the ice crystals.

3 Whisk the egg whites until stiff but not dry. Fold lightly but thoroughly into the partly frozen granita. Return to the container and freeze for 2–3 hours until firm. Serve decorated with redcurrants.

alcohol free	
citrus free	
dairy free	✔
gluten free	✔
wheat free	✔

strawberry and lychee sorbet

Serves 4 – Preparation time: 15 minutes, plus freezing – Cooking time: 15 minutes

Per serving – Energy: 290 kcals/1238 kJ · Protein: 2 g · Carbohydrate: 75 g · Fat: <1 g · Fibre: 5 g

400 g	**(13 oz) can lychees in light syrup, strained and juice reserved, lychees halved**
175 g	**(6 oz) caster sugar**
125 ml	**(4 fl oz) water**
750 g	**(1½ lb) strawberries, hulled**
1	**tablespoon lemon juice**

1 Put the halved lychees and juice in a saucepan. Heat gently for 5 minutes, then process in a blender until fairly smooth.

2 Put the sugar and water in a clean pan and heat gently until the sugar has dissolved. Bring to the boil and simmer for 3 minutes. Remove from the heat and allow to cool.

3 Process the strawberries in a blender with the lemon juice, adding the cooled sugar and water syrup as you blend. Sieve to remove pips and stir into the lychees.

4 Transfer the mixture to a plastic container and freeze for 1 hour. Remove from the freezer, beat the mixture to break up any crystals and freeze for a further hour. Repeat the beating and freezing, then freeze until firm.

5 Remove the sorbet from the freezer about 15 minutes before serving, in order to allow it to soften slightly.

alcohol free	✔
citrus free	
dairy free	✔
gluten free	✔
wheat free	✔

glossary

ALLERGEN: A normally harmless substance or food that in someone with a tendency to allergy provokes an allergic reaction.

ALLERGIC RHINITIS: A condition with similar symptoms to hayfever caused by an allergic reaction.

ANAPHYLACTIC SHOCK: A severe and life-threatening allergic reaction most often provoked by eating or by contact with a food to which the person is allergic.

ATOPY: A tendency to allergy.

BRONCHIOLES: The smallest airways in the lungs.

BRONCHODILATORS: A group of drugs that widen the bronchioles.

BRONCHUS: The airway in the lungs; the plural is bronchi.

CORTICOSTEROIDS: A group of drugs that mimic the action of hormones and which are produced by the cortex of the adrenal glands. Usually known simply as steroids.

DANDER: Scales shed by animals' skin, fur, hair or feathers. Dandruff is a type of dander.

DECONGESTANTS: A group of drugs used to alleviate nasal congestion.

EOSINOPHILS: A type of white blood cells involved in allergic reactions.

HISTAMINE: A body chemical that produces inflammation in an allergic reaction.

HYDROSYLATE: A type of baby milk formula in which the cows' milk proteins are modified to avoid producing an allergic reaction.

IMMUNOGLOBULINS: A type of blood proteins produced by the immune system. Also known as antibodies.

LEUKOTRIENES: A group of messenger chemicals produced as part of the immune response.

LYMPHOCYTES: A type of white blood cells involved in the immune response.

MAST CELLS: A group of cells of the immune system that produce histamine.

OTITIS MEDIA: Inflammation of the middle ear. Chronic secretory otitis media is usually known as glue ear.

PEAK EXPIRATORY FLOW: The maximum speed at which air flows out of the lungs.

PEAK FLOW METER: A device that measures the maximum speed at which air flows out of the lungs.

PERENNIAL RHINITIS: Rhinitis that can occur at any time of the year or all year round.

PLEURA: Membranes lining the lungs.

RHINITIS: Inflammation of the mucous membrane of the nose.

SEASONAL ALLERGIC RHINITIS: Another name for hayfever.

SPIROMETRY: A test which measures the rate at which air is exhaled and its volume.

TRACHEA: The windpipe.

index

index

127

FRONT COVER TOP LEFT

Octopus Publishing Group Ltd./Peter Myers

FRONT COVER CENTRE LEFT

Octopus Publishing Group Ltd./Neil Mersh

FRONT COVER CENTRE RIGHT

Octopus Publishing Group Ltd./Ian Wallace

FRONT COVER BOTTOM RIGHT

Octopus Publishing Group Ltd./Gary Latham

BACK COVER

Octopus Publishing Group Ltd./Gary Latham

Bubbles 31, /Chris Rout 71

Corbis UK Ltd./ Yann Arthus-Bertrand 48 Right,
/Craig Aurness 25, /Angela Hampton 7 Top Right,
/Jennie Woodstock/ Reflections Photolibrary 4
Centre Below, 27, 32–33, 34 Top Left, 36 Top Left,
38, 40

Octopus Publishing Group Ltd. 48 Left, /Martin
Brigdale 73, /Jean Cazals 14 Bottom Left, /Graham
Kirk 117, /Sandra Lane 2–3 Bottom, /David Loftus
66 Bottom, /Sandra Lousada 17 Top Right, 18
Bottom Left /Leo Mason 51 Bottom, /Neil Mersh 3
Bottom Right, 5 Centre, 76, 78, 80, 81, 82, 87, 91,
93, 94, 100, 102, 105, 110, 113, 120, 121, 122,
/Sean Myers 66 Top, 74 Top, 119, /Bill Reavell 57
Top, /Simon Smith Front Cover Bottom, Back Cover
Bottom, 5 Centre Below, 84, 98, 101, 103, 106,
112, /Grant Symon 89, 96 /Richard Truscott 51 Top,
/Ian Wallace 65 Top, /Philip Webb 74 Bottom, 92,
114, 115, /Polly Wreford 4 Bottom, 42, 46, 50.

Angela Hampton/Family Life 20, 44, 59 Top
Right, 61 Top.

MediTrack 37 Top Left.

Photodisc 2–3 Top, 4 Centre, 4 Centre Above, 5
Centre Above, 8–9, 10 Top Left, 13, 14 Top Left,
16, 18 Top Left, 22, 24 Top Left, 24 Bottom Centre,
39 Top Right, 62, 64, 68, 72.

Science Photo Library 39 Bottom, /James King-
Holmes 21, /K.H. Kjeldsen 19, /Dr. P. Marazzi 7 Top
Centre, 30 Bottom Left, 30 Bottom Centre, /Prof. K.
Seddon & Dr. T. Evans, Queen's University, Belfast
26 /David Scharf 28, /Hattie Young 65 Centre Right.

Stone/Ron Alston 17 Bottom Left, /Leland Bobbe
15, /Peter Cade 29, /Kindra Clineff 57 Bottom,
/Cyberimage 55 Bottom, /James Darrell 49, 59 Top
Centre, /Mark Douet Front Cover Top, Back Cover
Top, 1 /Gary Holscher 4 Top, 6, /Ian Logan 61
Bottom, /Gerard Loucel 47, /Peter Mason 5 Top, 52,
54, 56, 58, 60 /John Millar 37 Top Right, /Laurence
Monneret 10 Bottom Right, /Pat O'Hara 41, /David
Rosenberg 55 Top /Paul Sisul 11, /Chad Slattery 12,
/Steve Taylor 14 Centre Left, /Jerome Tisne 35.

Safety Note

Food Solutions: Asthma and Allergies should not be
considered a replacement for professional medical
treatment; a physician should be consulted in all
matters relating to health, particularly in respect of
pregnancy and any other symptoms which may
require diagnosis or medical attention. While the
advice and information in this book is believed to
be accurate, neither the author nor publisher can
accept any legal responsibility for any injury or
illness sustained while following the treatments
and diet plan.

acknowledgements